PLANTS IN HAWAIIAN MEDICINE

BEATRICE H. KRAUSS

ILLUSTRATED BY
MARTHA NOYES

3565 Harding Ave, Honolulu, Hawai'i 96816
(808) 734-7159   fax (808) 732-3627   besspress.com

Design: Carol Colbath
Kauna'oa on cover courtesy of David Yearian

Library of Congress Cataloging-in-Publication Data

Krauss, Beatrice H.
    Plants in Hawaiian medicine /
Beatrice H. Krauss; illustrated by Martha
Noyes.
            p. cm.
    Includes illustrations, bibliography, index
    ISBN 978-1-57306-034-9
    1. Medicinal plants - Hawaii.
2. Ethnobotany - Hawaii. 3. Hawaiians -
Medicine. 4. Plants, Useful - Hawaii.
I. Noyes, Martha, ill.
DU624.65.K71 2001   996.9-dc20

Printed in the United States of America

Contents

Acknowledgments

There is no question that Martha Noyes's beautiful drawings "make" this book. *Mahalo nui loa*, Martha.

I wish to thank Dr. Charles Lamoureux, director of the H.L. Lyon Arboretum, University of Hawaiʻi at Mānoa, for his *kōkua* in making available the assistance of two staff members: Karen Shigematsu, who provided various plants to be used for drawing the illustrations, and Toki Murakami, who typed several of the drafts of the text. *Mahalo* to you, too, Karen and Toki.

John Obata and Ron Fenstemacher made special trips to the central and northern Koʻolau Range summit areas to obtain specimens of the native *laukahi,* for which I am very grateful. *Aloha* and *mahalo*, John and Ron.

Thank you too, Peter Uroom, for bringing me both "live" and herbarium specimens of *Sargassum echinocarpum*, known locally as *limu kala*.

The staff of Hoʻomaluhia Botanical Garden played host on several occasions so that Martha Noyes could examine plants for her illustrations. Many thanks to all of you.

And special thanks to Derral Herbst for his review of the botanical references.

Preface

In Hawaiian medicine, plants are used in the healing process, and this treatment is known as herbal medicine. Although this healing process in Hawaiian culture includes *lomi* or *lomi lomi* (massage), *lua* (laying on of hands), and prayers and rituals, this book is concerned with the plants used and their preparation for medicine.

In old Hawai'i, before foreign contact from the West, Hawaiian healers had hundreds of native plants, in addition to those they had brought with them from the Marquesas, for use as medicine. However, there is record of probably not more than a hundred at most known today as having been used for medicine. Many, if not most of these, along with some postcontact introduced plants, are now used in what has primarily become folk medicine.

Thirty plants, frequently used in both old Hawai'i and today, have been selected for this book. An illustration and a physical description are provided for each plant, along with descriptions of general and medicinal uses, both in early Hawai'i and today.

 Introduction

The story of medicine begins the same the world over: primitive, i.e., original, peoples use for medicine those plants they consider to have healing properties. The Hawaiians, in contrast to Westerners, who favor the "trial and error" theory, believed that "the original knowledge of the healing qualities of various [plants] used has always been and still is revealed by ancestors, 'aumākua, in dreams" (Handy, Pukui, and Livermore 1934).

The person gathering, preparing, and administering the medicinal herb(s) is known by various names, depending upon the culture. In Hawai'i, he was called kahuna la'au lapa'au (the professional who practiced healing with plants).

A young boy became an apprentice to an established kahuna la'au lapa'au, studying with him for up to twenty years. During that period he had to learn the names of the plants to be used, where they grew, what part(s) to harvest, preparation of the plant material(s), formulations, dosages, etc. But this was not all he had to learn, for of as great or even greater importance were the rituals and prayers that accompanied every step on the way to the final administration of the prepared herb(s). While this was training for the "professional" practitioner, it was also part of the knowledge of priests.

We do not know how many medicinal herbs there were for the early Hawaiian practitioner to choose from among the thousands already growing here plus those the Hawaiians had brought with them. Handy, Pukui and Livermore mention the number 317.

All the parts of a plant were used for medicine—not necessarily from the same plant but when considering all plant material used: leaves, stems, roots, flowers, fruit, seeds, bark, and exudates such as resin. Most frequently, a medicine consisted of a formulation involving up to as many as ten different plants. Invariably, salt and *'alaea* (red or orange clay—iron oxide), both of them of therapeutic value (as astringent, counterirritant, and prophylactic) were added to such formulations.

Many medicines were prepared in the form of tea(s). Since hot water is therapeutic in itself, administering the medicinal herb in a hot tea enhanced the medication. Almost all one-plant medication was in the form of teas.

The medicinal material(s) was also administered as an extract obtained by mashing the plant material(s) and squeezing out the sap (juice), or as a suffusion created when spring water was added to the mash in order to extract the sap more thoroughly. The first of these methods produced a stronger solution than the second, which, however, extracted more of the active ingredient(s). Or the plant material was chewed and then processed as the material above.

The liquid (sap or juice) was squeezed from the macerated (mashed) plant material with a piece of the fabriclike sheath of young *niu* (coconut, *Cocos nucifera*) fronds (leaves). This material is light-colored and covered on both sides with extraneous material ("gook"). This was scraped off, leaving a material somewhat resembling cheesecloth (used today to squeeze juice from macerated plant material). The cleaned stem fibers of a native (indigenous, i.e., one that grows in more than one land but because of long separation has assumed a character unique to each area) sedge, *'ahu'awa* (*Cyperus javanicus*) was used to strain the extract or suffusion described above.

A special mortar and pestle, fashioned of basalt (lava) rock and reserved for use only in the preparation of medicinal herbs, was used to break up or mash plant tissue.

Fresh spring water was brought to the place of preparation in long-necked gourds kept for that purpose. Other gourds in the form of bowls were used to mash some formulations and to mix various ingredients. For measuring quantities of ingredients and dosages, "cups" consisting of half *niu* shells and two sizes of *'opihi* (limpet) shells were used.

Whereas in modern Western medical practice, medicine is administered in pills (including capsules), liquids, or injections so that prescriptions include instructions to take a certain number of pills, or so many teaspoons, tablespoons, or some other liquid measurement, in old Hawai'i the dosage was expressed as the amount of plant material: e.g., so many leaves or flower buds; or in size of a plant part: e.g., a piece of bark the size of a hand; or a quantity measured: e.g., an *'opihi* shell full.

Timing of medication was much as in Western medicine to the extent that medicinal preparations were administered, e.g., "twice a day, morning and evening" for a certain period of time.

The diet of the patient during the period of medication was controlled to some extent, and the period of medication ended with a special food, usually, but not always, seafood.

With the coming of the Westerners, the *kahuna la'au lapa'au* and apprentice system disappeared as such, and what remained was a kind of folk medicine, with Hawaiians and then people of other origins using various herbs (plants) for healing, remembering in part what the trained healer had practiced. Individuals who had sat at the feet of a grandparent learned what he or she had, in turn, learned from a grandparent. Thus knowledge that might have been lost was preserved in part

It is from among these people and those whom they have trained that the practitioner of today has come. By definition of the work, he or she might be called a *kahuna la'au lapa'au*. However, I agree with Handy, Pukui, and Livermore, who, in 1934, wrote that "although there are today older [and younger, I would add] persons, men and women who have considerable skills for prescribing remedies, there is probably no one in the islands whose knowledge of pharmaceutics and pathology would have qualified him [or her] for the title of *kahuna la'au lapa'au*." To this I would like to add that I find the more appropriate names to use, today, "practitioner" or "healer," also respectful and names to honor.

Today, after a period of skepticism on the part of many people, including Western-trained physicians, about the value of plants in the practice of healing, and a lack of support of the practice of herbal medicine on the part of government officials, there is increased spread of interest in and use of this type of healing on the part of the public and more support from regulatory agencies.

Of the thirty plants included in this book, only four have been scientifically proved to have curative ingredients: *'awa* (*Piper methysticum*), *'awapuhi kuahiwi* (shampoo or wild ginger, *Zingiber zerumbet*) *noni* (Indian mulberry, *Morinda citrifolia*), and *'ōhi'a ai* (mountain apple or Malay apple, *Syzygium malaccense*). Scientific research is continuing, which we hope will bring credence to practices followed by the Hawaiians for these many years.

Cautionary Note

This book is for those interested in the use of plants for medicine as one facet of Hawaiian culture; it is not intended as a *materia medica*—a manual to be used by the inexperienced reader. Further, the illustrations are artist's renderings and as such may not be botanically correct or useful for exact identification. I take this opportunity to warn readers against self-medication with herbs, and advise them to seek the services of a recognized practitioner. Remember, too, that there is still no scientific evidence available for the curative effect of many of the plants being used for medicine in Hawai'i.

The publisher, author, illustrator, and their heirs assume no liability for the results of any medicinal use of the plants described in this book.

ʻAwa

Hawaiian name: *ʻAwa*
Scientific name: *Piper methysticum* G. Forster

'*Awa* belongs to the pepper family, Piperaceae. Its name is derived from the Greek word for pepper, *perperi*, which in turn was derived from an Indian word.

Many of the members of this family are aromatic, including such spices as culinary pepper.

'*Awa* was introduced to Hawai'i from the Marquesas by the Polynesians, the first settlers. It was widely planted and persists in shaded, moist valleys, spreading vegetatively.

◆ Description

'*Awa* is a large, open-branched shrub from four to twelve feet tall, with pronounced "jointed" stems, i.e., with prominent ("swollen") nodes, and internodes of various lengths, depending upon the variety. The color of the stem also varies with the variety (see later descriptions of varieties).

The leaves, large and roughly heart shaped, are about five to eight inches long and nearly as wide at their greatest width; they are arranged alternately along the branches. The leaf blade has eleven to thirteen prominent, palmately arranged veins; i.e., they all originate at the base of the leaf and curve to approach one another at the tip. The petioles (leaf stems) are about an inch long.

Male and female flowers are borne on separate plants, on narrow spikes.

'*Awa* has an extensive root system, with individual roots attaining considerable size in older plants.

General Uses

'Awa is known as *kava* in other parts of the Pacific and in the pharmaceutical industry. In the South Pacific, notably in Samoa, Fiji, and Tonga, *kava* is served in a drink at special elaborate ceremonies, as well as used for medicine. Hawaiians did not observe this ceremony, but they did offer a *niu*-shell cup of *'awa* drink to a visitor, e.g., one chief visiting another, as a sign of hospitality, much as the Japanese offer a cup of tea. There are also reports of *'awa*-drinking social gatherings of men. To offset the unpalatability of *'awa*, a small variety of banana was eaten as a *pūpū*. This word *pūpū* has come to mean an hors d'oeuvre to be eaten with a pre-meal drink.

 ## Medicinal Uses

 ### Ancient

Although there were many forms (cultivars) of *'awa*, having suffixes such as *kua, hua, kumakua, mākea* and *mamaka*, those used primarily for medicine had such suffixes as *hiwa*, with long "black" internodes; *mō'i*, with short, dark green internodes and "whitish" nodes; *mokihana*, with shortish, yellowish green internodes, and an aroma resembling the aniselike aroma of the famous Kaua'i *mokihana*; *nēnē*, with dark spots on the internodes resembling those on the native goose of the same name; *papa 'ele'ele*, with short internodes, which also are spotted; and *papa ke'oke'o*, the most common of the *'awa*, with short internodes and dark spots. In general, Hawaiian practitioners seem to have preferred plants with dark, so-called black "skin," and therefore it might have been that 'awa hiwa was the most favored form.

Insomnia. 'Awa is frequently reported to be a narcotic, but it is not; it is a sedative or relaxant. It is because of these latter properties that a prime use of 'awa is as a cure for insomnia.

The cleaned 'awa root (the part of the plant with the highest concentration of the active ingredient) was cut into pieces and chewed or pounded. The macerated or mashed pulp was mixed with niu "water" (the liquid [endosperm] in the nut). This mixture was squeezed and the liquid thus obtained was strained through 'ahu'awa. To the cleared liquid was added sap squeezed from the bases of young kī (ti, Cordyline fruiticosa) leaves.

Thrush ('ea, a fungal disease primarily of children). The fibrous material remaining after squeezing the macerated 'awa root (see above formulation) was reduced to ashes by burning it over a fire. These ashes were mixed with ashes made by burning pili (a grass, Heteropogen contortus) and the "broiled-to-a-crisp" kukui (candlenut tree, Aleurites moluccana) nut kernels. These ingredients were well blended, and the mixture was smeared on the lining of the child's mouth and tongue where the lesions occurred. This treatment was repeated three times a day for five days. The child was also given drinks of ko'oko'olau (beggar's tick or beggar's lice or Spanish needle, Bidens pilosa, Bidens spp.) tea.

Kidney disorders. For kidney disorders, 'awa was prepared in the usual manner, i.e., chewed or pounded to a mash. To this was added another mash prepared by pounding lau kī (ti leaves). The whole was then squeezed and strained in the usual way. The liquid obtained was drunk before eating each morning and evening meal. Several drinks of fresh spring water helped to counteract the unpalatability of the 'awa.

Chills. The 'awa root, properly cleaned, was cut into pieces, beaten to a pulp (not quite to a mash). To this was added a small amount of spring water, and the mixture was allowed to stand for a short period. Then this mixture was pounded together with leaves and leaf buds of 'ōhi'a 'ai, a kernel of a green kukui fruit, leaf buds of ko'oko'lau and the juice of kō kea (a variety of sugarcane with a white rind). All these ingredients were well mixed and pounded together into a mash to which spring water was added. This concoction was strained through 'ahu'awa stems and, if necessary, further strained through a piece of the fabriclike sheath of a young niu frond. This liquid was drunk three times a day for three or four days. Because of the unpleasant taste of this medicine, a preparation of banana fruit or sugarcane was given.

"Splitting" headache. One or two pieces of properly prepared, i.e., cleaned, 'awa was cut into smaller pieces and chewed a few pieces at a time, once every half hour. After each half-hour chewing was completed, the residue was spat out. This was followed by chewing a piece of broiled niu "meat" to counteract the taste of the 'awa.

▨ Contemporary

A drink to alleviate insomnia has been made for many years in Hawai'i, under the name of kava. It is usually made from imported 'awa from Samoa, Tonga, or Fiji. This product is sold locally primarily in health food stores and has been used by people of various ethnic backgrounds. Dry, ground-up root has been available in two grades: a cheaper crude form containing extraneous material, and a more expensive better grade consisting of uniform, fine-grained powder.

The powder is added to water and the mixture is shaken; the powder stays in suspension since it is not soluble. (Orange juice is preferable to water since the orange juice "masks" the rather unpalatable taste of the *'awa*, besides adding a "bonus," namely vitamin C.) Attempts are now being made to produce a soluble form of *'awa/kava*.

Several years ago, the State of Hawai'i Department of Health, instigated by the Food and Drug Administration (FDA), removed the imported *kava* products from stores and prohibited further sales. I was told that the action was taken because an FDA official had found a statement to the effect that "the drinking of *'awa* causes scaly skin and bloodshot eyes." Actually, this phrase was out of context; the original reference reads: "*When taken in excess* [author's emphasis], the drinking of *'awa* causes scaly skin and bloodshot eyes." Excessive amounts are not prescribed in medicinal use of *'awa*.

For a period of time, then, no *'awa* was available in stores. (I'm sure, however, that individuals continued to bring it into Hawai'i.)

Recent calls to the State Department of Health and the local FDA office indicate that the order to prohibit sales of *'awa* or *kava* preparations has never been rescinded. However, a recent call to three stores indicated that "small *kava pieces* [author's emphasis] which are *brewed into a tea*" [author's emphasis] or "small *chunks* of *kava*" [author's emphasis] and "*kava* pills" are available. Thus commercial outlets in Hawai'i have circumvented the "ban" by selling *'awa* in a different form. There is also a question in my mind as to how effective "kava pills" are; their usefulness could depend on the mode of manufacture.

There is a report that early astronauts were supplied with *'awa* or *kava* instead of "traditional" sleeping pills because *'awa* or *kava* use had fewer side effects. This is an interesting example of an ancient primitive medicinal practice adopted in a highly technical modern technological operation!

It is ironical that a harvester of "wild" *'awa* has collected roots of this plant, "chipped" them and shipped them from Hawai'i to German pharmaceutical firms for over fifty years, while the plant's use as a medicine was largely ignored here, until fairly recently, when its use has gained popularity.

The leaves of *'awa* continue to be made into a tea.

ʻAwapuhi kuahiwi

Hawaiian name: *ʻAwapuhi kuahiwi* or *ʻawapuhi*
Common name: Shampoo or wild ginger
Scientific name: *Zingiber zerumbet* (L.) Sm.

'Awapuhi kuahiwi (literally "wild ginger," to distinguish this plant from other gingers), or *ōpuhi* (a shortened form of *'awapuhi*), was introduced by early Polynesian immigrants and is now naturalized. It forms a rather dense, luxurious ground cover in lower damp forests on all Hawaiian islands where such forests occur.

Description

This ginger forms clumps of two-foot-tall plants with about twelve narrow leaves four to eight inches long and two inches wide, arranged alternately along vegetative stems. The leaves are thin and more or less hairy on the underside. The stems rise from extensive, tubular, branched, knobbed, aromatic underground stems called "rhizomes." These rhizomes resemble the so-called "roots" of the culinary ginger (known in Hawai'i as *'awapuhi Pākē* [Chinese ginger] or *'awapuhi 'ai* [edible ginger], *Zingiber officinale*) sold in local markets and used extensively in Asian cooking.

In late summer, a flowering stem, about a foot tall, rises from the rhizome, separate from the leaves. The flowering head (inflorescence), oblong in shape, two or three inches long, consists of overlapping bracts (modified leaves), green and tinged with pink to red, which hide small, inconspicuous yellowish flowers, only one or two of which bloom ("open") at a time. The mature flower head is full of a sticky, slimy ("soapy"), aromatic liquid (sap). The plant "goes dormant" in the winter for about three or four months after flowering, with the leaves turning yellow and dying. New leaves rise from the rhizomes in the spring.

General Uses

The sap was used by the ancient Hawaiians as a shampoo, hence its common name. Persons of many ethnic groups still use this sudsy liquid for shampoo, especially when going to swim in a forest pool. Passing through strands of this ginger, one pulls up a flowering head, administers a shampoo, and jumps into the pool. Local children engage in "shampoo ginger battles" (and have for many years). A pulled-up flowering stalk becomes a club with which to swat another child over the head, resulting in a stream of "soapy" juice pouring over the hapless victim's face.

The underground stems, especially, and the leaves also, were used to scent *kapa* (tapa).

This ginger is also grown in various botanical gardens and arboreta and by many individuals who specialize in growing native plants.

 Medicinal Uses

 Ancient

Bruises, cuts, and sores. In early days, *'awapuhi kuahiwi* was used as a compress to apply to "sore spots" as well as on bruises and cuts on arms and feet. The ashes made by burning leaves in a fire were finely ground and mixed with ashes from the *'ohe lau li'ili'i* (native bamboo, *Schizostachyum glaucifolium*). To this mixture of ashes were added the milky sap from the kernel of green *kukui* fruit (nut) and the sap of the rhizome of the ginger. These were mixed and well blended. This concoction was placed on the injured area and held in place, if necessary, with a strip of *kapa*, which served as a bandage.

Headache. Pieces of the underground stems, to which *pa'akai* (Hawaiian sea salt) had been added, were pounded into a mash, placed on a piece of the fabriclike sheath of a young *niu* frond, and squeezed. The resulting strained liquid was drunk and the fibrous residue, in the form of a "medicine ball," was rubbed across the forehead, care being taken to prevent any of the material from entering the eyes.

Toothache. Small pieces of a rhizome of *'awapuhi kuahiwi* were partly roasted by rotating them over embers. Such a prepared piece was placed on the top of the aching tooth and the patient was instructed to bite down on it, causing a liquid to ooze over the tooth and adjacent gum. If the pain did not subside with one application, the treatment was repeated until the pain ended.

Ringworm. Two pieces of a rhizome of *'awapuhi kuahiwi*, the size of a thumb; two taproots of *'auko'i* (coffee senna, *Senna occidentalis*); and four pinches of *pa'akai* were pounded together with an *'opihi* shellful of urine. This mixture was squeezed in a piece of *niu* frond sheath, and the liquid obtained was rubbed on the affected spots. The application was made three times a day until this fungal infection disappeared.

Various other skin diseases. Two taproots of *'auhuhu* (a strand plant belonging to the legume, i.e., pea family, also used as a fish poison, *Tephrosia purpurea*) were added to the above concoction, but without the urine. This mixture was used for various other diseases, including skin ulcers.

Achy joints. A formula containing both flower buds and rhizomes of this ginger, bark of *'iliahi* (sandalwood, *Santalum* spp.), and leaf buds of *'auhuhu* was used for achy joints. These plant materials were pounded together into a mash, and the liquid (sap) was squeezed out. A hand dipped into this liquid was rubbed on the sore spots. This treatment was repeated morning and evening for a week.

Sprains. A mixture of the rhizomes of this *'awapuhi;* *'awa* root; a leaf of *'ilie'e* (a native plumbago, *Plumbago zeylanica*); and a ripe *noni* fruit were mixed with a little water and mashed. The juice (sap) was squeezed from this concoction and rubbed on the affected areas three times a day: morning, noon, and evening.

Stomachache. There is no reference in the several texts on Hawaiian medicinal plants on the use of *'awapuhi kuahiwi* for stomachache. However, there has been mention made in the past and present about the use of this plant for that purpose. That this is so is not surprising considering that ginger has for centuries been known for its anti-inflammatory property. The Hawaiians would have pounded the rhizome of *'awapuhi kuahiwi* into a mash, added fresh spring water, strained the mixture, and drunk the resulting liquid.

❖ Contemporary

The above is much the procedure used today, except that the rhizomes are more likely to be placed in a blender to be ground up, and strained through cheesecloth or a sieve instead of a piece of cleaned *niu* frond fabriclike sheath. *'Awapuhi 'ai* is more frequently used than *'awapuhi kuahiwi* because of the greater availability of *'awapuhi 'ai.* The medicinal value of the two gingers is similar.

This reminds me of my mother's treatment for

stomachache for my three siblings and me. She would reach into our medicine chest and bring out a bottle labeled "Jamaica ginger" (made in Jamaica from the culinary ginger, *'awapuhi 'ai*). We disliked taking it since it was strong and biting; we complained, but the effect seemed miraculous—no more stomachache! I like to think: "Separated by thousands of miles, thousands of years apart, yet one healing practice."

Hala

Hawaiian name: *Hala* or *pūhala*
Common name: Screw pine
Scientific name: *Pandanus tectorius* S. Parkinson ex Z.

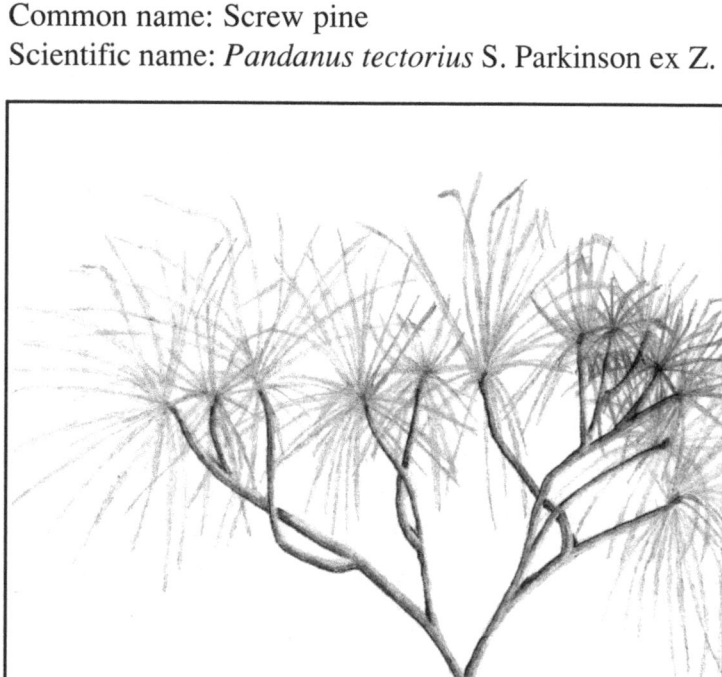

Hala has been, until recently, known as a Polynesian-introduced plant, i.e., brought to Hawai'i by its original settlers from the Marquesas. Then, recently, a fossilized drupe (fruitlet) was found in a piece of dislodged lava. The lava flow predated the arrival of the Polynesians, so now we call *hala* an indigenous species. Of course, the Polynesian settlers may well have brought *hala* too.

Although *hala* is primarily a lowland plant, it grows at elevations up to two thousand feet. It forms large groves, such as, for example, the extensive "royal" grove still standing in Hāna; unfortunately, this grove was diminished somewhat when the Hāna airport was built. *Hala* trees also grow together in lesser groves in valleys and on hillsides, or scattered singly or in clumps.

Description

Hala is a wide-branched tree, twenty feet tall or more, and is characterized by its few or many straight, cylindrical aerial or "prop" roots. The surface of these roots is covered with small protuberances that are actually dormant rootlets. The prop roots continue to grow in the air (hence the name "aerial" roots), eventually entering the soil, where the above-mentioned "abortive" rootlets start to grow, forming a root system operating in the same manner as the original root system. They are called "prop" roots because once they have entered the soil they support the branches, which have great clusters (bunches) of leaves at their ends. These are so heavy that without these support roots the acutely angled branches would break. The tender meristematic (growing) tip of a prop root, prior to its entry into the soil, is protected by a cuplike sheath consisting of layers of paperlike material. This sheath is closely fitting, but can be easily removed by twisting. It disintegrates as the prop root enters the soil.

The trunk and branches are conspicuously marked with "rings," which are the scars left by the clasping, spirally arranged bases of leaves that have fallen. The leaves (*lau hala*) are long and narrow, three to six feet long and two to four inches wide. The expanded base clasps and encircles the branch stem, and the tip is pointed. The margins and the prominent midrib on the underside of the leaf have prickles (sharp-pointed spines).

The fruit consists of fifty or more angular, wedge-shaped yellow-to-orange-to-red fruitlets called "drupes," "phalanges," or "keys," because if one is removed or falls out of the composite fruit, the remainder are easily removed. Thus the first drupe to come out is the "key" to the removal of the other drupes. Each drupe (*pua hala*) is about two inches long and about one inch wide. The outer end is solid and woody. It contains four to twelve cells, which are either empty or contain one seed each. The inner end is fibrous with some fleshy tissue. The seeds are nutlike and tasty.

Male and female inflorescences appear on different trees. The female inflorescence consists of a cluster of closely appressed flowers that develop into a composite fruit (called a "sorosis" after the Greek word). The fruit is globose (rounded), about eight to ten inches in diameter, or ovoid (somewhat elongated), about eight inches long. It looks like a pineapple and is sometimes pointed out as such to tourists by tour guides. Because of this appearance, the synonym for *Pandanus* is *ananas*, which is both the scientific name and, in several foreign languages, the common name for pineapple.

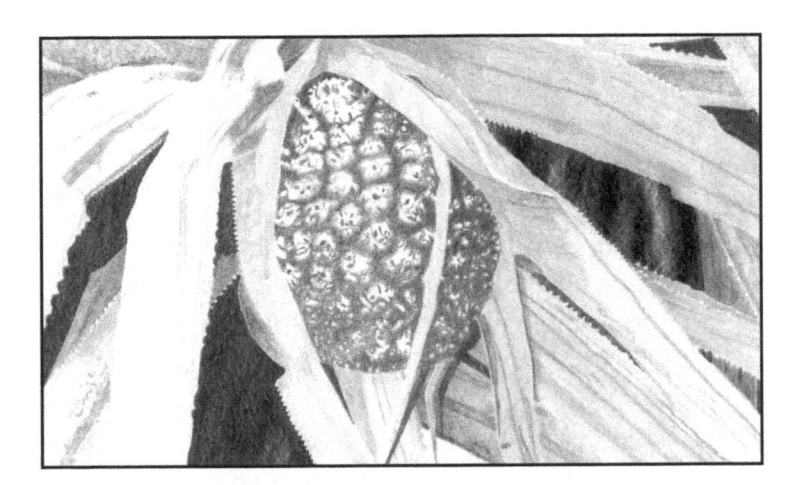

 General Uses

The leaves of *hala* were the most important part to the ancient Hawaiians; their many house and other mats used for the floor, bedding, and sails for their canoes were plaited from strips of prepared *lau hala*.

Because of the fragrance of the fleshy ends of the drupes of immature fruits, they were, and still are, used to make highly prized *lei*. When the dried flesh at the inner ends of the old drupes was teased away from the fibers, the exposed fibers served as a brush to paint designs on *kapa*, with the outer woody portion forming the brush handle.

 Medicinal Uses

 Ancient

Thrush and other childhood diseases. The following formulation was prepared specifically for children from one to six weeks old, but the same formulation was probably altered for older children by increasing the amount of *hala* plant material used. This is one of the few examples in which only one ingredient was used in a medicinal formulation in old Hawai'i. Most formulations included parts of several to many plants.

Hala drupes (probably only the soft inner portion) that had been cleaned and dried were chewed into a pulp and placed in the child's mouth, and then the child was nursed. This treatment was given twice a day, once in the morning and once at night.

Chest pain. The formulation for a medicine to treat chest pain required eight different plants: the tips of aerial roots of *hala;* leaves (probably) of *pā'ihi* (a native nasturtium related to watercress, *Rorippa sarmentosa*); the barks of the taproots of *pōpolo* (glossy nightshade, *Solanum americanum*) and *'uhaloa* (waltheria, *Waltheria indica*); flowers and leaf buds and older leaves of *'uhaloa*; stems of *'ala'ala wai nui pehu* (*Peperomia* spp., belonging to the pepper family); the bark of the *'ōhi'a* stem (probably *'ōhi'a 'ai*); ripe *noni* fruit; and *kō kea*. These were all pounded together into a mash and the resulting concoction squeezed through *'ahu'awa*. The cleaned liquid was heated with red-hot rocks and then cooled. The cooled mixture was taken as a drink twice each day, once in the morning and once in the evening.

Difficult childbirth. A multiplant formulation was prepared for difficult childbirth. Tips of aerial roots of *hala;* leaves (probably) of *pohepohe*, or *pohe* (the marsh pennywort, *Hydrocotyle verticillata*); *kohekohe* (a red sedge, *Eleocharis* spp.); the white base of young *hala* leaves; stems of *'ala'ala wai nui pehu*; leaves and fruit of *'ihi mākole* (a sorrel with red stems, *Oxalis corniculata*); leaf buds of *naio (*bastard sandalwood, *Myoporum sandwicense*); "meat" from a *niu*; and *kō kea* were all pounded together into a mash and the squeezed-out liquid left to stand for a while. Then it was strained and heated with hot stones. The patient was made to lie face down and was given the liquid to drink twice each day, once in the morning and once at night.

Hau

Hawaiian name: *Hau*
Scientific name: *Hibiscus tiliaceus* L.

Hau, a strand plant (one that grows primarily near the sea), is a many-branched tree that grows to a height of twelve feet or more. Two types are reported for Hawai'i: one of medium height, an erect tree with a gnarled, crooked trunk; and the more common variety, in which the branches spread parallel to the ground, forming what appears to be an impenetrable dense thicket of trunks and branches.

The leaves are a rounded heart shape, from two to eleven inches in diameter. They are leathery to the touch, with margins either entire (without teeth or notches) or notched. The upper surface is smooth, but the undersurface is whitish due to the presence of fine hairs that form a mat over the underside of the leaf.

Hau flowers profusely; the blossoms appear at or near the tips of branches. The flowers resemble those of other members of the family genus *Hibiscus*. The buds are two to three inches long, and open in the morning into bright yellow "cups," most forms of which also

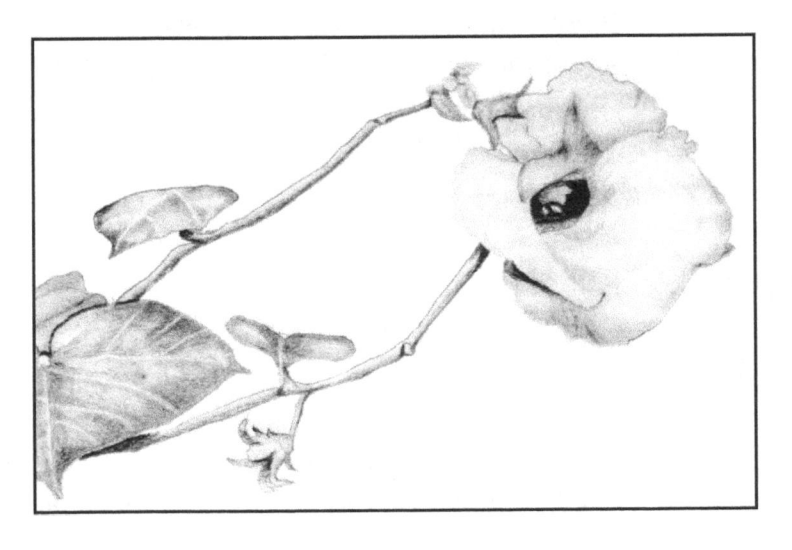

have a maroon center. Later in the day, the petals change to a dull orange and by nightfall become a dull red. The following morning the dull red corolla (the petals cup) lies on the ground, having detached from the calyx (the outer row of flower parts) cup. The downy (covered with minute hairs), five-toothed calyx cup, which is persistent (remains on the flower stem), is about an inch long and is accompanied by ten or twelve shorter bracts (narrow, leaflike structures). The seeds are contained in a fruiting capsule that develops from a superior ovary, which remains enclosed by the calyx when the corolla falls. The capsule has five valves (chambers), each of which contains several smooth seeds.

 ## General Uses

When the wood of the *hau* is dry, it is very light in weight and tough. Because of these characteristics, it was used for the cross-sticks of kites, for fire "drums" used to produce fire by rubbing with a harder wood such as *olomea* (*Perrottetia sandwicensis*), and (also because of its buoyancy) for outriggers of canoes. Strips of the fibrous inner bark of the stems were braided or twisted into an attractive satiny cordage.

 ## Medicinal Uses

Ancient

Constipation. The use of *hau* as a medicine depends on the presence of a slimy sap. This occurs in all parts of the plant but is found chiefly in flower buds and ovaries and in the stems. These parts were used as a laxative, especially for children, but also by adults.

In one formulation for children from three days to four weeks old, flower buds (no number specified) were used; from five weeks to three months the dose consisted of the ovaries of eight flower buds; from four to eight months, twelve ovaries; and from nine months to one year, sixteen ovaries. After two years of age (including adults), flower buds of a relative, *pūwahanui*, were used instead of *hau*.

For constipation not controlled by a laxative, the sap of the bark was used. The bark complex was stripped from the stem, and the flesh on the inner side was scraped off with an *'opihi* shell. These scrapings were allowed to stand in a *niu* shell. Spring water was then added and the resulting hard mixture, after standing for another period, was strained through *'ahu'awa*. This concoction was drunk at night. After that the patient rested until daybreak, when he or she was given a drink made by crushing ripe *noni* fruit, adding water, and heating with red-hot stones. When the liquid had cooled, it was strained through a piece of the prepared sheath of young new frond. The resulting clear liquid was used as an enema.

Chest congestion. The sap scraped off the inside of a piece of bark stripped from a *hau* branch was hand-mixed with the slimy sap from young fronds of an unknown plant (reported as *'uwī'uwī* [*Conyza* spp.], but probably *'iwa'iwa* [*Asplenium* spp.]), and *kikawaiō* (a native fern, *Christella cyatheoides*). Spring water was added, and the slimy liquid was strained through *'ahu'awa* stems. Next, the barks of mature roots of *'uhaloa* and *pōpolo* were pounded to a mash and mixed. The mixture was squeezed through a piece of prepared fabriclike sheath material from *niu*. The liquid obtained from this straining was added to the slimy liquid first described. This was drunk, followed by a tea made of *ko'oko'olau*.

For women in labor. The inner bark of the *hau*, with its slimy sap, was soaked in spring water. The resulting liquid was drunk by the mother to ease labor pains and facilitate labor. Some of the liquid was also rubbed on her stomach.

Dry throat. Young leaf buds of *hau* were chewed into a fine mash and swallowed. This was followed by a mouthful of spring water. This medicine was taken twice a day, morning and night.

▨ Contemporary

Young buds and flower ovaries of *hau* are still used as a laxative. There is no preliminary preparation; they are simply chewed and swallowed.

'Ilima

Hawaiian name: *'Ilima (lei)*
Scientific name: *Sida fallax* Walp. cultivar

Although *'ilima lei* (the flower of a domesticated, i.e., cultivated, form of *'ilima* that was strung to make *lei* both in ancient and contemporary Hawai'i) is known to have been used for medicine by ancient Hawaiians, it is probable that other forms of *'ilima* (native) were the ones actually used for medicine.

Description

'Ilima lei is a large, branched shrub that grows up to four feet high. The leaves, about an inch long, are oblong, with a somewhat blunt tip and scalloped margins. The flowers are yellow (other forms of *'ilima* have orange or red flowers). They are about an inch across and occur singly, or two or three together, on stems near the tips of branches. The seed cases (capsules) are seven- to twelve-spoked, wheellike, and beaked, with one seed per "compartment." The leaves and seed cases are covered with a whitish down.

General Uses

This *'ilima* was and still is used primarily for making *lei*. Buds are picked in the morning to string. It takes up to one thousand buds to make a neck *lei*. In old Hawai'i, *'ilima lei* were reserved for the *ali'i* (royalty). Often, *maile* is interwoven with an *'ilima lei.*

Medicinal Uses

Ancient

Thrush. A combination of the bark of *'ilima lei* taproots; *'uhaloa* flowers and leaf buds; *'ala'ala wai nui pehu* flowers and leaf buds; flowers, leaf buds, and leaves of *pōpolo;* ripe *noni* fruit; and *kō kea* were pounded together to a mash, strained, placed in a calabash, and allowed to stand. This liquid medicine, for children at least two years old, was taken as a drink three times a day.

Asthma. The flowers, leaf buds, and bark of the taproot of *'ilima lei;* the bark from the taproots of *pūkāmole* (a low shrubby native plant, *Lythrum maritimum*); and *kō kea* were pounded together into a mash. This material was then squeezed and the liquid obtained was strained into a gourd calabash. The mixture was heated in the usual manner, and when it had cooled, it was taken as a drink twice a day, once in the morning and again in the evening for five days, with the patient lying down while drinking the mixture.

Constipation. A mild laxative for babies was made by squeezing out the sap from mashed *'ilima* flowers.

Birth pains. During painful birth the mother was given *'ilima* flowers to chew and swallow.

Kalo

Hawaiian name: *Kalo*
Common name: Taro
Scientific name: *Colocasia esculenta* (L.) Schott

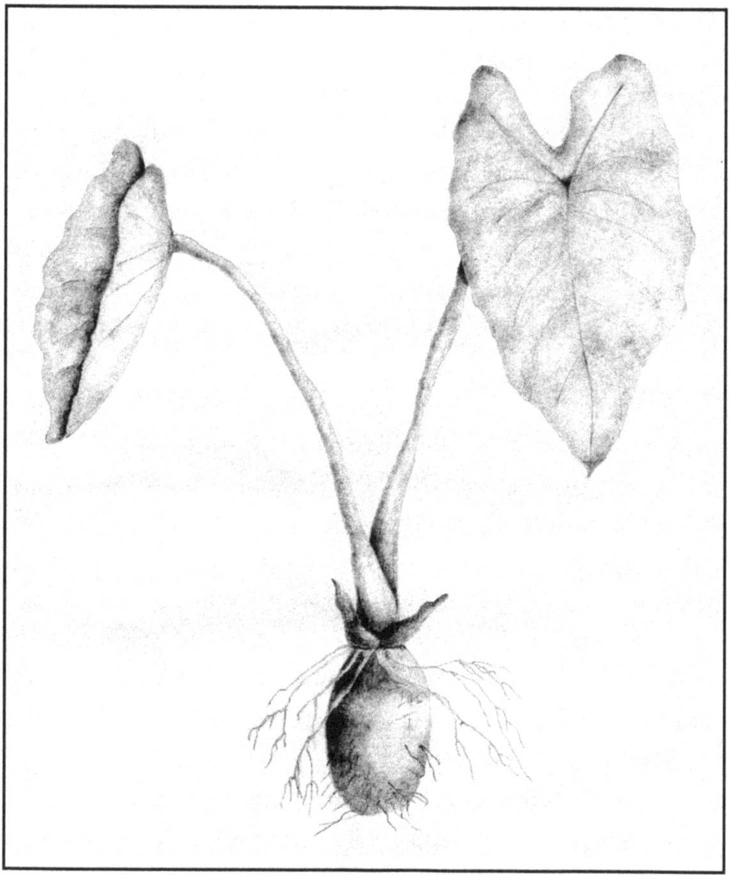

Kalo was perhaps the most important plant in ancient Hawai'i, primarily because it was the staple food, i.e., the most important carbohydrate food, as rice is for Asians and white (Irish) potatoes are for Europeans.

Perhaps as many as a dozen varieties of taro were brought by the Polynesians who came from the Marquesas to settle in Hawai'i. Yet when Handy, in the 1920s, collected varieties still growing here, and about which the older Hawaiians knew, he found that there had been over two hundred varieties at one time, most of which were mutants ("sports") originating from the original ones they had brought.

Of these original varieties, Handy found about seventy, of which about fifty are still preserved in various collections, including Lyon Arboretum.

 Description

Kalo is a perennial herb (one that grows for longer than a year), one to three feet tall, with a cluster of smooth heart-shaped leaves arising in a cluster from a tuberlike underground stem, erroneously called a "root." Botanically, this underground stem is called a "corm."

The corm is about the size and shape of a large white potato. The "skin" is rough and dark. The interior (flesh) is tough, rather dense, and fibrous. Its color may be white, yellow, pink (reddish), or bluish lavender. True roots emerge from it, and buds are present (as on aboveground stems, which develop into shoots called *'ohā*; these sometimes mutate to form new varieties).

The leaves are up to two feet long and up to one and a half feet wide at their greatest width. They may be a dark or light green; suffused with dark purple; or blotched with white. The petioles are long, even longer than the leaf blades. They are attached to the underside of the blade slightly inside its margin. They are light green, red (pink), dark purple (almost black), and sometimes spotted or striped. The top of the petiole is bent so that the tip of the leaf (blade) points down. The last-formed leaf lies furled within a groove on the next-youngest leaf.

The *kalo* inflorescence resembles that of the ornamental caladium (to which it is related). It consists of an open yellowish-white (cream-colored) tube (bract), constricted below the middle and enclosing a long spike covered with small flowers. The flowers are sterile at the tip and middle, with fertile male flowers between and fertile female flowers below. A number of fruits with seeds form from some of the female flowers.

All parts of the plant have special cells, larger than those in surrounding tissue, that contain bundles of needlelike crystals of calcium oxalate called "raphides." If any part of the plant is taken into the mouth raw, the walls of these cells rupture and the crystals are released explosively, lodging in the lining of the mouth and tongue and causing great irritation. Heat (by baking or boiling), denatures the protein of the cell walls so that the crystals are released gently and therefore do not stick into the mucous membrane.

 General Uses

The main use of taro was and is for food, primarily the beaten corm (*poi*), but also unbeaten and in a dessert. Taro became an offering to be placed on an altar if the preferred offering, fish, was not available. Dyes for designs to be stamped on *kapa* came from the cut ends of leaf stems. *Poi* was used as a paste to join pieces of *kapa*.

Medicinal Uses

Ancient

Although all varieties of taro probably could (and would) have been used in medical *'apu* (doses), Hawaiians in old Hawai'i seem to have preferred varieties with the suffixes *'ula'ula* (with red corm flesh), *'āpi'i* (not described), *mana* (not described), *hāpu'u ke'oke'o* (leaf stalk and flesh of corm white), *uahi-a-Pele* (blackish leaf stalk and dark-colored *poi*), *manini* (leaf stalk striped like *manini* fish and white corm flesh and *poi*), *'apuwai ke'oke'o* (water collects on its blades; cooked corm and *poi* are whitish and corm flesh is crumbly), *haokea mana* (has two leaf tops, which, along with flesh of corm, are white), and *pi'iali'i* (leaf, petiole, and *poi* are all reddish).

Only uncooked flesh of the taro corm was used in medicinal formulations (these must have been difficult to take with those miserable needlelike calcium oxalate crystals!). Formulations containing scraped corm tissue served as purgatives to be given in connection with other medicines "to ferment in the stomach." As stated in an old herbal medicine text: "The illness goes inside of the body of the sick person and the *'apu* goes after it and catches the illness, then the problem is over."

Two different preparations of such *kalo* medicines are given here:

1. The skin was removed from a corm and the latter

washed well with water. Enough of the corm flesh was scraped off to fill a *niu*-shell cup. Two and one-half sections of *kō kea,* the flesh of a ripe *niu,* and two overripe *noni* fruit were mixed together and pounded to a fine mash. The liquid of this mixture was squeezed into a gourd calabash and the taro scrapings were added. If the resulting liquid began to thicken, the *kō* was chewed (again) to make the concoction "smooth" again. Then the liquid was strained in the usual manner. Five *'apu* of this medicine were drunk; adding the flesh of *kā'e'e* (*Mucuna gigantea*) bean pods to the medicinal drink increased its purgative effect. Steamed *lū'au* (taro leaves) and *palula* (cooked sweet potato leaves) were eaten in conjunction with this medication.

2. The taro corm was peeled, washed, and scraped to produce three-fourths of a *niu*-shell cupful. To this was added the milky sap from four green *kukui* nuts (this may mean either the sap that collects in the depression left in a green *kukui* fruit when it is broken away from its fruit stem or an extract of the mashed kernel from an immature ["green"] *kukui* nut). Fresh spring water was added until enough liquid was produced to drink when the mixture was squeezed in the usual way. The juice produced by squeezing was strained as always. Another concoction consisted of half a section of *kō kea* and one-fourth of the flesh of a ripe *niu.* These were pounded to a mash, and the juice was squeezed out. This juice was added to the first juice (squeezed from taro corm and green *kukui* nuts, described above), and then well blended to produce the medicinal drink, which was taken on five successive mornings. Broiled or steamed sweet potatoes and some *palula* were eaten with this drink.

Cylinders cut from peeled and washed taro corms were used as suppositories in cases of severe constipation. Just as men in more modern times use a styptic

stick to stop the bleeding and start the healing process
when they cut themselves shaving, the ancient
Hawaiians stopped the bleeding and started the healing
process of any cut by cutting a section of a taro leaf stem
and applying the sappy (oozing) surface to the cut.

Contemporary

Today, I doubt anyone would take a medicine consisting
of raw taro corm scrapings. However, the cut end of a
petiole is still used to stop bleeding of a cut and hasten
its healing (also a painful process, if not as painful as a
mouth-administered dose).

Kauna'oa

Hawaiian name: *Kauna'oa*
Common name: Native dodder
Scientific name: *Cuscuta sandwichiana* Choisy

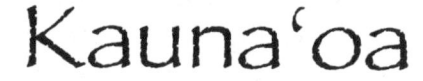

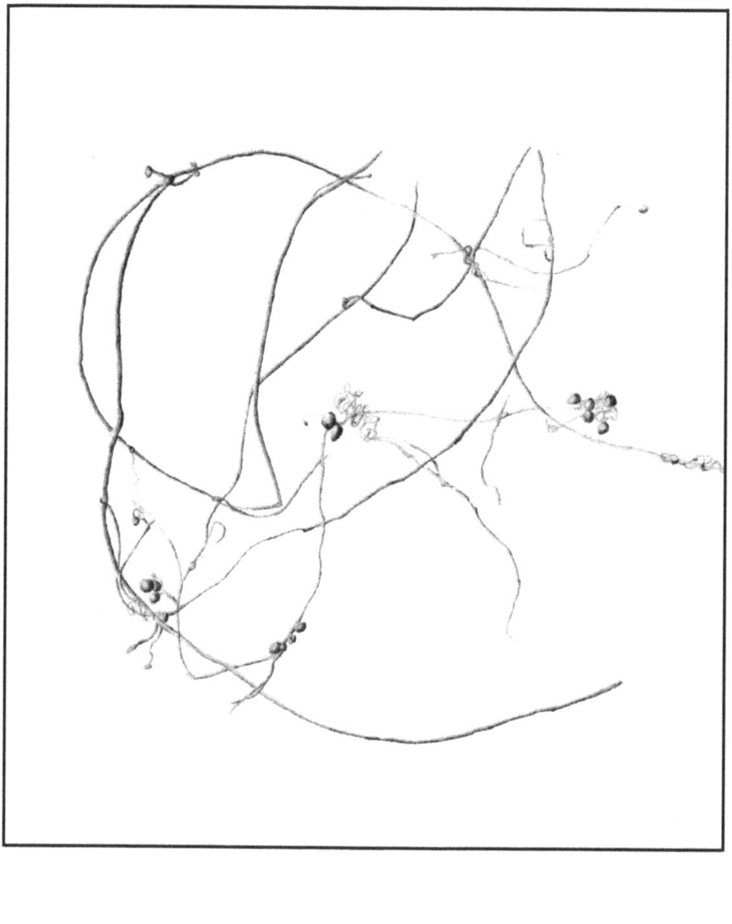

Kauna'oa is a native (endemic, i.e., growing only here) plant. It is parasitic, obtaining its nutrition by attaching itself to other plants (hosts) by means of haustoria ("suction cups"). *Kauna'oa* is usually found in coastal areas, where its hosts include both native and nonnative plants.

Kauna'oa derives its genus name, *Cuscuta,* from the Arabic word *kusku,* meaning "tangled twist of hair," which the plant resembles, and its species name, *sandwichiana,* from the Sandwich Islands, the first European name for the Hawaiian Islands.

 Description

Kauna'oa consists of usually unbranched, slender, threadlike yellowish orange stems without leaves. Although juvenile plants have small roots, these disintegrate rapidly, so that mature plants are rootless and the plants are therefore not connected to the ground.

The flowers are very small, in compact clusters. Fruits are capsules containing one to four tiny dark reddish brown seeds.

 General Uses

Kauna'oa was and is still used for *lei.*

◈ Medicinal Uses

◈ Ancient

Chest cold with thick phlegm. One man's hatful (a post-contact measurement) of *kauna'oa* and one woman's hatful (a postcontact measurement) of *moa* (a medicinal herb, *Psilotum nudum*) were chopped into small pieces and to that mixture were added four ti leaf buds. All were pounded to a fine mash. A *niu*-shell cupful of fresh spring water was thoroughly mixed in. The juice was squeezed from the concoction and strained in the usual way. After a quantity of the liquid was drunk, the patient, after resting for a while, was tickled with a chicken feather to induce vomiting. Presumably, the phlegm vomited from the stomach had originated in the lungs and had passed into the stomach.

For women after giving birth. A cupful of *kauna'oa* (pressed down to fill) was pounded to a fine mash and mixed with a *niu*-shell cupful of fresh spring water. The *kauna'oa* and water were well mixed and the liquid squeezed out and strained in the usual manner. This liquid was given to a woman after she gave birth to help discharge the placenta and remove accumulated blood.

◈ Contemporary

Kauna'oa is not as frequently used for medicine today as it once was, but is still used to remove phlegm from the stomach.

Kī

Hawaiian name: *Kī*
Common name: Ti
Scientific name: *Cordyline fruticosa* (L.) A. Chev.

Ki was brought to Hawai'i by the Polynesians who were the first settlers. It commonly grows at the lower edges of forests and in hanging valleys (the smaller valleys on the eroded sides of larger valleys), preferring moist, semishaded areas, but it also grows in open, drier areas if irrigated. Many cultivars (cultivated varieties) have been created; these have very colorful leaves.

Description

Ki is a shrubby plant that reaches a height of twelve feet and is usually unbranched. If the upper part of the stem with leaves is cut off (topped) for some use, the remaining stem forms two branches from terminal buds. The slender stem (and branches, if present) is closely ringed with leaf scars (the basal leaves turn yellow, then drop and die), and ends in a cluster of leaves arranged in a close spiral at the top or ends. It resembles a feather duster.

The leaves are long and narrow, from one to three or four feet by three to six inches wide. Both their upper and lower surfaces are smooth, shiny, and flexible and have a prominent midrib on the underside. The petiole is two to six inches long and is deeply channeled.

The panicle (loose cluster of flowers), about a foot high, rises from the center of the leaf cluster. Flowers are small and numerous, lilac-tinted, each about a third of an inch long, cut halfway down into six rolled-back segments. Only a few berrylike fruits develop from the many flowers. The berries range in color from green to yellow to red and contain seeds.

The *ki* plant has a long taproot, which in old plants grows to a considerable size.

General Uses

In old Hawai'i, *kī* was a very valuable plant because of its many uses. It was, and still is, grown around houses to ward off evil and bring good fortune. The detached plant with its long stem and cluster of leaves is said to have been the prototype of the later-day version of the feathered standard, the *kāhili*, with its long handle (usually made of bone) and the terminal cluster of feathers. This later version and, supposedly, the original *kī* "*kāhili*" were emblems of royalty.

The leaves were used on fishnets for *hukilau* and for such diverse articles as wearing apparel (rain capes and sandals); house thatch; whistles; wrapping or packaging for gathered fruits or *lei* or other offerings (known as *pū'olo*); *lei* worn by priests; and while still attached to the stem, toboggans to slide down hills and slopes.

The baked root was eaten as a sweet. After Western contact, an alcoholic drink, *'ōkolehao*, was made from the root.

The plant is now extensively used in landscaping.

 ## Medicinal Uses

Ancient

Growths in the nose. *Kī* flowers; *kī* and *'ōlena* (turmeric, *Curcuma longa*) rhizomes; and, after contact, the rhizomes of *'awapuhi ke'oke'o* (*Hedychium coronarium*) were mixed together and pounded to make a mash. Water was added and the whole was mixed by hand and squeezed; only the resulting liquid was saved. The liquid thus obtained was strained in the usual way. Dry powder from *naio* was scattered on the liquid and mixed in.

A *hāpu'u pulu* "ball," consisting of a quantity of *pulu*, the golden, silky hairs covering and protecting the last-formed, still-furled frond at the top of the stem of the native tree fern, *hāpu'u* (*Cibotium glaucum*), was wrapped in a piece of special *kapa* known as *māhuna*, dipped into the prepared liquid, and inserted into the nostril(s) to be inhaled. After Western contact, a small amount of the alcohol made from *kī* root was added to the formulation. The process of inhalation was repeated five or six times.

Asthma. A disease reported as "difficulty in breathing," assumed to be asthma, which Dr. O. A. Bushnell (personal communication) reports as being a "possible" disease of precontact Hawaiians, had several cures. For one of these formulations, flowers of *kī* and the starchy pith inside the trunks of *ama'u* (a native fern somewhat resembling the common *hāpu'u, Sadleria cyatheoides*) and of *ēkaha* (bird's nest fern, *Asplenium nidus*) were pounded together, mixed, repounded, the liquid squeezed from the concoction, strained in the usual manner, and mixed with *poi* made either from *kalo* or *'uala* (sweet potato, *Ipomoea batatas*). After the medicine was taken, a purgative was given.

Later, a second dose of the asthma medicine was taken, along with broiled *lū'au*, to which *'inamona* (a relish or condiment made from the roasted kernels of *kukui* nuts) was added, accompanied by a tea brewed from *ko'oko'olau*. The tea was taken four or five times.

Another medicine for asthma was made by using both the flowers and leaf buds of *kī*; overripe *noni* fruit; enlarged roots of *'uala*; a species of *Peperomia*; and *kō kea*. It was prepared by pounding until the leaf buds of *kī* became soft. Then added to this were scrapings of tissue from the underside of the blades of *kī* leaves. This *na'a* (scrapings of leaf bases of *kī* leaves, a definition from one of the old books on Hawaiian medicine; the word does not appear in the Pukui-Elbert dictionary) is mixed with the *ki* leaves, water, and the scraped flesh of *'uala* storage roots. This mixture was squeezed and strained in the usual manner and then taken as a drink. If the first drink was ineffective, water was added to the residue, which was squeezed, strained, and made into another drink and drunk.

This medicine sometimes caused vomiting. A lot of vomiting was considered to be a good sign.

Dry fever, lack of perspiration. *Ki* leaves were stripped of the blade on either side of the midrib (torn, beginning at the tip of the leaf), and the two pieces tied together and wrapped around the head. Another set was tied around the chest, under the arms, and sometimes, a third joined pair was tied around the abdomen. The *ki* leaves were dipped in a calabash of cool spring water (and redipped as the water evaporated and the leaf warmed) to enhance the soothing effect.

This method of alleviating the discomfort of a fever is reminiscent of my mother's manner of treating the fevers we four children occasionally had. She would fold a small terry cloth towel lengthwise to form about a three- or four-inch-wide band, which she dipped into a bowl of cold water and then placed on the child's forehead (and how wonderful it felt!). When the towel dried and became warm, she would dip it again in the cool water and reapply it. Same procedure, and the same results, but the Hawaiian way used only the products of nature, while for my mother's method she needed manufactured materials and machine-cooled water. Either way, the result was that the patient felt better.

Generally, after treating the patient for fever as described above, the Hawaiian prescription was followed with a purgative; a drink of some kind; steamed *'uala* storage roots or broiled *kī* leaves; and a tea made from *koʻokoʻolau* leaves.

Tuberculosis. Narrow short strips resulted when the blades of both green and the older yellowed *kī* leaves were torn along the lines of the close, parallel veins. These strips were then torn from the midrib. The short, narrow strips were braided into a *lei* and worn by the patient for a day, a form of symbolism. The wearing of the *lei* was accompanied by a drink of *koʻokoʻolau* tea and a good meal. The result was a sound sleep.

Vaginal discharge. Flowers and leaf buds of *kī* leaves and stems of *ʻalaʻala wai nui pehu*; *ʻihi ʻawa* (an *Oxalis* species); tips of *hala* aerial roots; leaf buds and leaves of *pōpolo*; mature *noni* fruit; and *kō kea* were mixed together and divided into five equal parts, to make five doses. Then the ingredients were pounded into a mash, squeezed, and the resulting liquid strained in the usual manner. The clear liquid was then heated with red-hot stones, and when it had cooled, the patient, while lying down, drank it twice a day, morning and evening.

Backache. A heated flat stone was wrapped in a *kī* leaf and placed against the aching back.

◈ Contemporary

Leaves are still used to "soothe the fevered brow," and tissue scraped from the underside of the leaf is sometimes used as a compress or poultice.

Half-leaves are still placed around the head (forehead) to ease headaches.

Kō

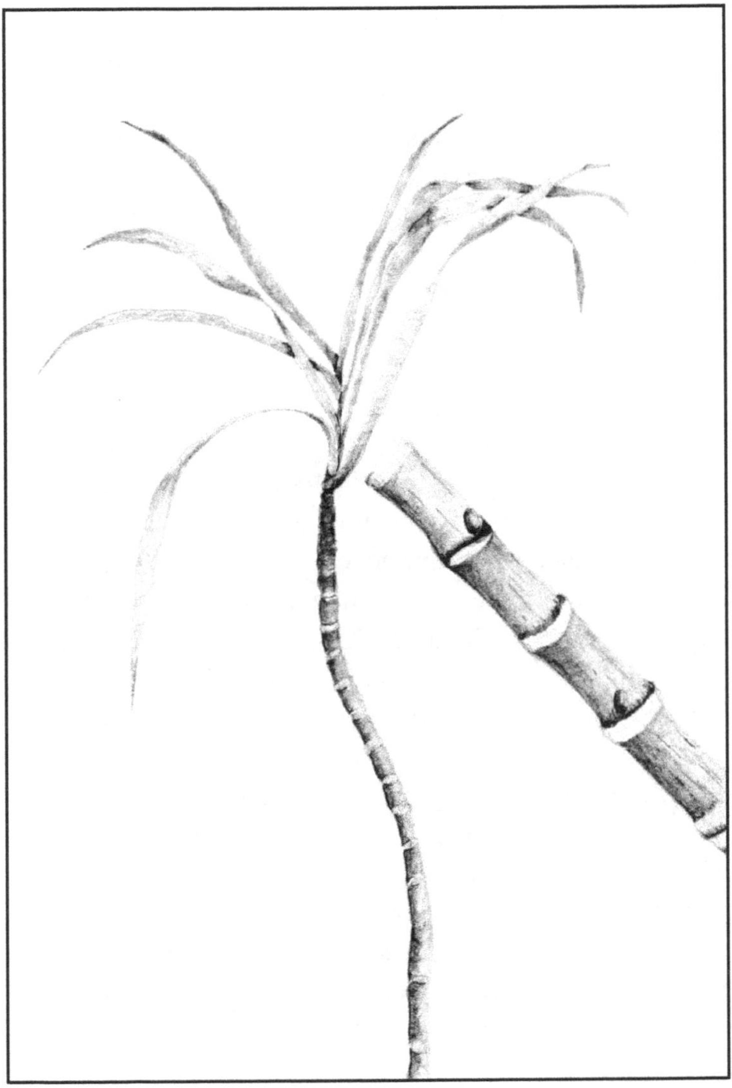

Kō is a giant perennial grass. The genus name is derived from the Greek word *sakcharon*, referring to the sweet juice, probably from the Malesian *singkaia*. The species name, *officinarum*, refers to the plant's use as a medicine. This species is known only in cultivation; it may have originated as a cultivar in prehistoric times in Southeast Asia or eastern India.

The Polynesians from the Marquesas, the first to settle in Hawai'i, brought several varieties with them. After the arrival of foreigners, these native varieties were crossed with varieties collected from other tropical countries to create hybrids. These became the commercial varieties grown on the many plantations in Hawai'i to create its prime source of economic wealth.

 ## Description

Sugarcane grows in clumps (called "stools") of single unbranched stems. The stems, or stalks, are coarse, thick, and, as noted, unbranched, up to fifteen feet tall or taller. The internodes are relatively short and prominent, an inch or more in diameter. A hard rind ("skin") encloses a solid, fibrous, juicy pulp. The rind, often striped, ranges in color from green to yellowish to dark purple— almost black. As the stalks increase in length and diameter, the plant has a tendency to lean.

The upper, younger leaves form a terminal cluster, while the older leaves, on the lower part of the stem, dry and hang, eventually dying and dropping off. The leaves are one or more feet long and one and one-half or more inches wide. Both surfaces of the blade are smooth except for the margins, which are sawtooth (very irritating to handle).

An inflorescence appears at the end of each stem in the fall months. It is in the form of a straight, wandlike, feathery rosy- to lavender-colored "tassel," one to two feet long. The tassel consists of many spikelets (branches and subbranches). The tassels turn a silvery color on maturity; flowering fields present a beautiful sight. Small seeds are formed.

 ## General Uses

The ancient Hawaiians used *kō* leaves for thatching their houses, although they were not as popular for this purpose as *pili* and ti leaves. The flowering stalk was used as a kind of arrow in a sport. Children were encouraged to chew pieces of the peeled ("skinned") internodes to "harden" their gums. The juice (sap) was extracted from the fibrous pulp and used to sweeten two desserts.

 ## Medicinal Uses

Ancient

Although the juice from *kō* was used primarily to make bad-tasting medicines more palatable, it has therapeutic qualities of its own.

Although, as already noted, the ancient Hawaiians had many varieties of *kō*, those most widely used for medicine were *kō honua'ula* (with red rind and pulp and long internodes), *kō kea* (with a white rind) and *kō lahi* (with a dark-colored rind).

Deep cuts and wounds. Four young *kō* leaf buds, two *koali pehu* (*Ipomoea alba*) vines, and one-fourth *niu*-shell cup of salt were pounded together to a fine mash and mixed. This mixture was bundled up on a piece of tapa and wrapped in a ti leaf. This bundle was then broiled until the contents were cooked. When cooled sufficiently, the concoction was placed on the cut or wound. (The Hawaiians were a stoic people to tolerate a dressing of this composition!)

Fractured limb. The fractured limb was first set by supporting it with a dried stem of *mai'a* (banana, *Musa xparadisiaca*), and then the above-described concoction was "poured over" the area of the fracture. (My guess is that reference is being made to a compound fracture rather than a simple one.)

Contemporary

Kō is still primarily used to "sweeten," i.e., disguise, the bad taste of some medicines.

Koa

Hawaiian name: *Koa*
Scientific name: *Acacia koa* A. Gray

Koa, a magnificent tree considered the "monarch" of all Hawaiian trees, is native (endemic) to the high forests. Many legends are associated with *koa*.

Description

Koa trees grow very tall, reaching heights approaching one hundred feet, with crowns of far-reaching branches. When the trees grow in large groves on mountainsides, close together, the trunks, which may attain a diameter of as much as ten feet, are very straight and are without branches for as great a height as sixty feet. The bark on young trees is smooth and light gray, becoming very rough, i.e., furrowed longitudinally, in older trees. When polished, the wood from the trunk, often called Hawaiian mahogany, is beautiful—red, with a wavy grain.

The juvenile leaves, the first leaves formed after the seed germinates or if new growth appears after an injury to the trunk, are finely divided, consisting of five to seven pairs of pinnae (branchlets), each pinna with thirteen to twenty-four pairs of leaflets. Later leaflike

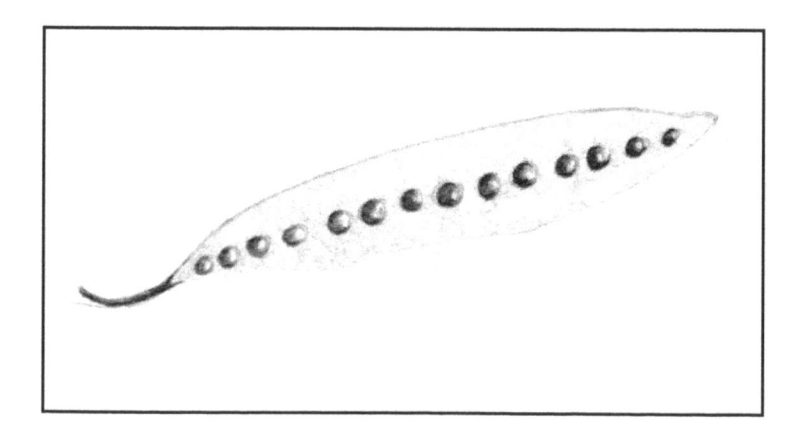

structures, actually petioles that have "flattened" (broadened" out), are called "phyllodes." They are crescent-shaped, stiff, smooth, and dark green.

The flowers are small, cream-colored, and packed in "balls" borne in clusters near the ends of branches. The fruit is a flat, thin pod.

 ## General Uses

The *koa* trunk was especially prized in old Hawai'i for making the great double canoes. It was also used to make calabashes for the storage of various materials, but not food because of the presence of a resin that affected the taste of food. When wooden musical instruments such as the guitar and *'ukulele* were introduced, *koa* was the favorite wood for these. Certain wooden carvings were also made from *koa*.

 ## Medicinal Uses

 ### Ancient

Fever or long confinement to bed. To induce sleep during fever or when the patient was sick long in bed, young *koa* leaves that had been pounded and crushed were spread to completely cover a sleeping pallet made of mats piled one upon another. This caused the patient to perspire, and he or she was able to fall asleep. Upon waking, the patient was given a drink of fresh spring water or perhaps a tea such as one made from *ko'oko'olau* leaves.

Thrush. One *'opihi* shell full of ashes obtained by burning *koa* (probably the "leaves") and one *'opihi* shell full of ashes obtained from burning the dried flesh of a mature *niu* were mixed with the milky sap of four green *kukui* nut fruits and well blended. This material was smeared on the lesions in the child's mouth twice a day, once in the morning and once in the evening. This medicine was used primarily for children from six months to one year of age.

Contemporary

Only ashes obtained from the so-called leaves are used today in various medicines.

Koali ‘awa

Hawaiian name: *Koali ‘awa* or *kowali ‘awa*
Common name: Morning glory
Scientific name: *Ipomoea indica* (J. Burm.) Merr

Koali, or *kowali,* is the general Hawaiian name for many different morning glories. The one referred to here, distinguished by the suffix *'awa,* is native (indigenous). As with most morning glories, it is a vine, this particular variety growing inland, in drier areas at lower elevations, and often growing wild over other vegetation.

 ## Description

Koali is a vine with a twisting stem, often more than fifteen feet long. The many-branched stem is fleshy at its growing end and woody in older parts, usually with a smooth exterior.

The leaves are usually entire, blades thin and broadly ovate (egg-shaped), and with smooth surfaces, although sometimes covered with minute hairs, especially on the underside. The petioles are as long as the blades.

The flowers usually occur singly, in the axils of leaves. They are funnel-form (bell-shaped), about two to almost three inches long, and blue or purple (rarely white), turning pink in the afternoon.

The fruit is a smooth brown capsule, often four-angled, or sometimes rounded or somewhat flattened at its apex. There are one to four seeds, dark brown, rounded, and smooth.

General Uses

Hawaiian legends describe *koali* vines as being used as ropes. In actuality, stout older vines were sometimes used in place of the more usual *niu* and other plant fibers. There is even report of swings made of *koali* vines.

 Medicinal Uses

Ancient

Constipation. *Koali* is best known as a purgative; all parts of the plant have this property. For this formulation, twenty flowers and twenty leaves of *koali* were used. A piece of the meat of a mature *niu* was pounded and added to the *koali* leaves and flowers, which had been left whole. This mixture was wrapped in *kī* leaves and broiled over charcoal embers. The cooked cocoction was eaten, followed by drinking two mouthfuls of the water from a mature *niu*.

After the purging effect had ended, the patient was given cooked fish or chicken to eat, along with *lū'au* and *'inamona*. Although there was a wild fowl in ancient Hawai'i, I believe that the serving of chicken and chicken soup was a postcontact addition to this practice.

The *koali* was not considered to have completed its "job" until a foamy material was passed, whereupon the patient was given a lot of fresh spring water and *ko'oko'olau* tea.

Wounds, sores, and broken bones. A perhaps even more important medicinal use for *koali* was as a poultice for wounds, sores, and broken bones. The bark of the roots and the vine itself (stems plus leaves) were crushed and mixed with salt. This dressing was then placed on the affected area. However, the combination of ingredients, especially the salt, caused an intensive burning reaction, so a *kī* leaf was usually placed between the wound and the poultice.

The stories of *koali*'s ability to heal broken bones are numerous and dramatic. After the bone was set, the poultice of mashed *koali* plant material plus salt was placed over the affected area (with the above-noted precaution of placing a ti leaf between the wound and the poultice) and bound on with a strip of *kapa* to hold it in place. It is assumed that the salt served as a counterirritant and the *koali* accelerated the blood flow in the area of healing.

The above-noted *koali* dressing was used not only for open wounds and sores, but also for bruises and especially sprains.

Thrush. The flowers and flower buds were used for *'ea* in very young babies, as early as ten days, when two flowers were used; and up to three weeks old or a little older, when up to four flowers were chewed and given to the baby.

▨ Contemporary

Koali, crushed or mashed, with or without salt, is still used rather often, primarily for sprains.

Ko'oko'olau

Hawaiian name: *Ko'oko'olau* or *kī nehe*
Common name: Beggar's tick or beggar's lice or
Spanish needle
Scientific name: *Bidens pilosa* L., *Bidens spp.*

Ko'oko'olau is the Hawaiian name for the precontact native *Bidens* species. When the Western species, commonly called beggar's tick (or beggar's lice) or Spanish needle, was "introduced" to Hawai'i, most probably as an "unintentional adulterant" of imported commercial seeds, the Hawaiians recognized its relationship to the native species, called it *kī nehe*, and substituted it for the native species they had previously been using in medicinal formulations.

 Description

There are nineteen species native (endemic) to Hawai'i. The ancient Hawaiians used this plant exclusively for medicine. It is probable that they used all the species, depending perhaps on availability and perhaps on the spiritual value of each species.

Ko'oko'olau is either an annual (grows new each year) or perennial herb or small shrub, one to two feet tall. Most of the species are erect and branched.

The leaves are arranged on opposite sides on the stem and are simple (occur singly) or compound (made up of smaller units called leaflets), with margins either entire or serrated (notched).

Inflorescences are on long petioles, borne terminally at the tip of the main stem and at the terminus (end) of lateral branches, or only on lateral branches.

The flower head consists of a disk covered with tiny flowers called "disk florets." The florets are perfect (have both sex organs) or have only the female organs. The flower disk is surrounded by yellow ray florets, which are sterile.

Fruit, called "achenes" (small, hard, dry fruit having

one seed with a thin outer covering that does not burst when mature) infrequently have awns (bristly hairs). The fruit is primarily linear, straight, curved, twisted, or coiled.

Kī nehe, the postcontact introduced species, has some of the characteristics of *koʻokoʻolau* described above. It is primarily characterized by the absence of or, in one variety, small, insignificant white or yellowish ray florets, and the prominent awns on the achenes. A similar species, *Bidens alba,* has recently become a very common roadside weed; it has prominent white ray florets.

Medicinal Uses

The prime use of both plants, *koʻokoʻolau* and *kī nehe,* was and is as a medicine. *Koʻokoʻolau* was used in the formulations below, until *kī nehe* was introduced. Then *kī nehe* was used in the same formulations, the Hawaiians having recognized the import as similar to their own varieties. To the gardener, *kī nehe* is considered an obnoxious weed.

Ancient

Thrush. For children from one to four weeks old, a few leaves and flowers were chewed by the mother and the macerated material transferred to the mouth of the child, followed by nursing. From five weeks of age on, increasing numbers of leaves were brewed in *niu* "water" to make a tea, which was given to the child to drink.

Constipation. The same formulation used for thrush was used to alleviate constipation.

Asthma. For severe cases of asthma, *ko'oko'olau* flowers, leaf buds, and older leaves; the leaves and fruit of *moa holokula* (not identified); flowers and leaf buds of *'uhaloa*; leaf buds and red blossoms of *'ōhi'a lehua* (*Metrosideros polymorpha*); and *kō honua'ula* were pounded to a fine mash, mixed, and placed in a gourd calabash. Then hot stones were added to heat the mixture. The concoction was cooled, the stones removed, and the remainder strained. A mouthful of this medicine was drunk three times a day for five days.

Tuberculosis. For tuberculosis, flowers, leaf buds, and green leaves of *ko'oko'olau*; fruit and leaves of *moa holokua*; fruit and leaves of *'ala'ala wai nui pehu*; *'ōhi'a 'ai* bark; leaf buds of the red-flowered *'ōhia lehua*; *kukui* flowers; kernels of *kukui* nuts "burned to a crisp"; "overripe" *noni* fruit; *'ihi mākole*; and *kō kea* were mixed and pounded into a mash. The liquid thus obtained was strained and heated. The liquid was drunk by the patient while he or she was lying on his or her stomach. The medicine was taken twice a day, morning and evening, until five doses had been taken.

As a tonic. *Ko'oko'olau* flowers, leaf buds, and leaves; *'uhaloa* flowers and buds; leaf buds from the red-flowered *'ōhi'a lehua* and *kō honua'ula* were pounded to a mash, mixed together, and placed in a gourd calabash. Spring water was added, and the mixture was heated with hot stones, and then covered until it cooled. The liquid was squeezed from the concoction and strained. A mouthful was drunk three times a day, before eating, for five days.

◼ Contemporary

A tea brewed from either fresh or dried *koʻokoʻolau* (more frequently) or *kī nehe* is used alone. In fact, there is at least one popular commercial *koʻokoʻolau* (probably *kī nehe*) product on the market labeled "Hawaiian tea." Of course anyone can gather leaves from plants in his or her own garden (where it is considered a weed), or those collected from roadsides or fields. A note of caution: it is important to find out whether the area where the *koʻokoʻolau* or *kī nehe* plants are growing has been sprayed with toxic herbicides; if so, do not use. Today the tea is generally taken as a tonic, i.e., to overcome that "blah, let-down feeling."

Kuawa

Hawaiian name: *Kuawa*
Common name: Guava
Scientific name: *Psidium guajava* L.

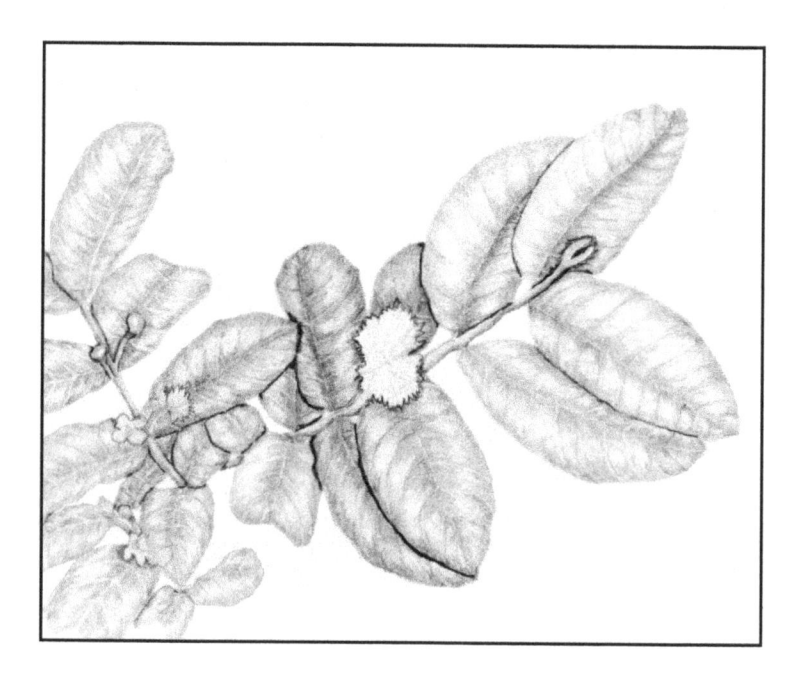

Kuawa is a "Hawaiianization" of the common name of this plant, guava. A postcontact plant, it is included in this book because the Hawaiians added it, soon after its introduction, to those native plants they were already using, and because it is still widely used by people of varied ethnic origins. In fact, some people think of *kuawa* as a native plant. Actually, it was introduced from tropical America and is now found along roads and in waste lands, from where it is grubbed out to clear land for farm crops. It is also grown in orchards as a commercial crop for the production of pulp and juice.

 Description

Kuawa is a large, low evergreen shrub or small tree, from six to twenty-five feet high, with wide-spreading branches that end in square (in cross-section) and downy twigs. The trunk is characterized by layers of smooth reddish brown bark that scales (peels) off in patches to expose a lighter inner bark; this results in a mottled pattern.

The blunt-tipped leaves, three to six inches long, vary from oblong to oval. They are a dull green, with a matte upper surface and an undersurface more or less hairy. Veins are prominent, forming a "feather" pattern.

The flowers are characteristic of the myrtle family, of which *kuawa* is a member. They are about an inch or more across. The calyx is bell-shaped, split irregularly to form lobes. There are four to six white petals; stamens are numerous and white, with yellow anthers. (Stamens include the male organs of a flower.) The flowers have a faint fragrance.

In shape, color, and size, the fruit most commonly

resembles the California lemon. At the flower end of the fruit are the dead, dark remnants of the calyx lobes. Inside the thin yellow skin of the mature fruit is a solid, usually pink, somewhat acid flesh. In the fruit's center is a juicier, less solid pulp filled with small, hard, kidney-shaped seeds.

Hawaiians distinguished several varieties as *kuawa lemi* (lemon guava), with sour flesh; *kuawa momona* (sweet guava), with sweet, white flesh and thicker skin and larger seeds than the other varieties noted here; and *kuawa ke'oke'o* (white guava), with white flesh.

 General Uses

The fruit is eaten fresh and is also processed into juice, jams, jellies, "butter," catsup, and many desserts and confections. The wood is used to make a high-quality charcoal and in some types of structural work.

Medicinal Uses

Ancient

In early Hawai'i, as well as today, the leaf buds and young leaves, exclusively, are used for medicine.

Diarrhea. For children from two to six months old, "four-plus-two" (a Hawaiian way of saying "six") leaf buds were chewed by the mother and transferred to the mouth of the baby. To "fortify" this antidiarrhea treatment, the child might also be given some prepared *pia* (Polynesian arrowroot, *Tacca leontopetaloides*), which in itself is a treatment for diarrhea. If the first treatment did not control the diarrhea, it was repeated. If the diarrhea was not even then controlled, a purgative was administered.

Dysentery. For a more serious type of diarrhea, i.e., dysentery, a mixture of the taproots of young *kuawa* plants plus the bark of some older ones; the white basal tissue of young *hala* leaves; and the "roots" (i.e., the corm, or underground stem) of *mai'a* were chopped into pieces, mixed well, and pounded into a fine mash. Fresh spring water was then added to the mash and "cooked" by placing red-hot stones in the calabash containing the concoction. This mixture would have been considered sufficiently "boiled" or "cooked" if the plant material had darkened considerably. Then the stones were removed and the calabash covered and allowed to stand until the mixture had cooled. It was then strained and drunk. The medicine was taken repeatedly until the dysentery was controlled.

Sprains. Leaf buds of *kuawa* and of *'auhuhu*; salt; and *kō kea* were mixed and pounded to a mash. This concoction was placed in a fabriclike sheath from a piece of prepared *niu* frond and squeezed over the injured limb. The treatment was repeated three or four times a day until the injury healed.

Deep cuts. The same medicine as above was poured on deep cuts to heal them. A description of the formulation was followed with the warning that the burning sensation was part of the cure.

As I have noted elsewhere, the Hawaiians in early years were a stoic people to have tolerated the application of this and some of the other medicine administered by their practitioners!

▨ Contemporary

Today, the chewing and swallowing of the macerated leaf buds, but primarily the young (pinkish) leaves of *kuawa*, is practiced by people of many ethnic groups, in addition to Hawaiians.

Well-macerated older guava leaves are applied to a wound such as a bad bruise or cut and bound into place. This treatment is especially useful on hikes in areas where guava bushes are available.

A tea made from young leaves or leaf buds is made to cure headaches.

Crushed leaves have even been used like smelling salts to revive persons who have fainted.

Kukui

Hawaiian name: *Kukui*
Common name: Candlenut tree
Scientific name: *Aleurites moluccana* (L.) Willd.

Kukui, now designated the state tree, was brought to Hawai'i by the first settlers, Polynesians from the Marquesas. They are large trees common throughout the islands, occurring primarily in the lower forest regions.

Kukui belongs to the spurge, or euphorbia, family, all members of which have an acrid (sharp, "puckery") sap, which in some members of the family is poisonous.

Kukui are particularly conspicuous in valleys and in hanging valleys (narrow valleys lining the sides of broader valleys like Mānoa), because of their light-colored foliage.

Description

The tree has a stout trunk, comparatively short, with a thick many-branched crown. The outer bark is light colored and somewhat rough in older trees. The main taproot is large, and many lateral roots are found close to or on the surface of the ground.

The leaves vary greatly in shape, from narrowly ovate (oval) to angularly lobed, which in an extreme case resemble maple leaves. The leaves may reach a length of eight inches or even more, with the width of the largest lobed leaves about equal to the length. The petiole is long. The surface of the leaves is covered with a "bloom" (a powdery or floury covering). *Kukui* gets its genus name, *Aleurites* (a Greek word meaning "floury"), from this leaf bloom. The bloom is also what gives *kukui* the pale green foliage that makes this tree so visible in the landscape.

The flowers, both male and female, occur together in large clusters at the ends of branches. The many individual flowers are small and whitish. Only as many as five (seldom more) fruits develop from flowers in each cluster. A single tree produces a large crop of seventy-five to one hundred pounds of fruit each year.

The fruit, about two inches in diameter, consists of a fleshy husk (covering), green when immature and gray-ish when mature. Within the husk lies the nut, which is the seed. The nut is enclosed in a parchmentlike cover-ing, which is much more persistent than the husk. The husk disintegrates soon after the mature fruit falls, but the covering remains around the nut for some time. The nut, or seed, when mature is flat on one side and domed on the other, with the surface shallowly ridged; it has a black "bony" shell when mature. The kernel within the shell is white and very oily; in fact, as much as 80 per-cent of the nut is oil.

General Uses

It is very fitting that *kukui* is Hawai'i's state tree, because it has so many uses. The flowers and leaves were and still are used for *lei*. The husk of the immature green fruit was used as a dye. When the whole nut cracked, it was placed over embers, the oil in the nut caught fire, and the soot from the smoke was collected for use as a dye for decorating tapa and painting the hulls of canoes. The shell of the nut was polished and strung to make *lei*. The whole kernel was used to make candles; it is this use that gives *kukui* its English name, "candlenut tree." The oil was expressed from the kernel and used for lamp oil and as the solvent for the *kukui* nut soot to paint designs on tapa and the hulls of canoes. The roasted kernel was made into the condiment *ina-mona*. From the inner bark of the trunk and exposed roots was made a common dye used to color *'olona* cordage and tapa.

 ## Medicinal Uses

▨ Ancient

Constipation. Because of the purgative effect of the raw *kukui* nut kernel, it was used in cases of severe constipation. If the purgative effect was too drastic and diarrhea resulted, the patient was fed a daub of *poi* on which had been placed a "lump" of prepared *pia*, which itself is used to control diarrhea. This combination was chewed until smooth and then swallowed, after which the patient took a drink of spring water.

Abscesses and similar infected sores. The affected area was first thoroughly washed with a liquid made by adding pounded *'ahakea* (a native tree growing in the mountains, *Bobea* spp.) to spring water. This mixture was boiled and strained.

Kukui kernels were dug out of immature (green) nut shells, wrapped in *kī* leaves, and broiled over embers until well done. When these had cooled, they were pounded into a fine mash. To this was added some of the milky sap of *'ulu* (breadfruit, *Artocarpus altilis*) and finely powdered *'ahu'awa* or powdered *lama* (a native [endemic] hardwood tree, a kind of ebony, *Diospyros* spp.). The whole was mixed thoroughly to eliminate lumps. This concoction was placed on the affected area twice a day, once in the morning and once in the evening, until the sore was healed.

General debility. *Kukui* nut kernels were placed in a wooden calabash and pounded to a mash, and then boiled taro leaves were added. The slimy "flesh" scraped from *kikawaiō* (a native fern) and some *kikawaiō* fronds were added to the still-hot contents of the wooden calabash and all were thoroughly mixed. The patient lay on his or her side and ate the concoction along with a meal consisting of fish and *'uala poi*, which had been mixed with *ko'oko'olau* tea. Additional tea was consumed along with meals twice a day, morning and evening, for five days.

▧ Contemporary

The mature kernel of the *kukui* nut is still used, today, as a cathartic or purgative. I was surprised one day when the nurse's aide taking care of my sister exclaimed with joy when she found I had a *kukui* tree in my yard and asked if she might collect some nuts on the ground beneath it. She was a native of Costa Rica, where this tree also grows and where the natives also use it as a purgative.

It has been reported that the sap from the green fruit (obtained as described above) is used for stomachache. Personally, I question the advisability of its use for this affliction.

The sap from green fruits is now used for chapped lips and canker sores, whereas the mashed kernel of immature nuts is rubbed on cold sores.

Laukahi

 Hawaiian name: *Laukahi*
Common name: Native plantain or broad-leaved
(common) plantain
Scientific name: *Plantago* spp., *Plantago major* L.

Native laukahi

An endemic and an introduced form are both called *laukahi* by the Hawaiians; they are both treated under this heading.

Laukahi is a member of the plantain family and in Hawai'i has several species, one of which (*Plantago hawaiiensis*) grows in dry to moister areas, often in cracks in lava, and another (*Plantago pachyphylla*) in wet forests. The latter species will be described since that is the one I grew, i.e., nursed for five years, in the greenhouse at the Lyon Arboretum.

Some characteristics of the two forms are similar. There is variation in morphological features within the species to be described, and the features here described are those of the specimen I grew. This plant came from the summit of the Wai'anae Range on O'ahu.

◈ Description

The stem is short and unbranched. Leaves are pale green, somewhat elliptical, and about eight inches long and three inches wide, narrowing in width toward the base, with veins convening slightly toward the base of the leaf. The apex of the leaf is blunt. Both upper and lower surfaces of the leaf are woolly (covered with hairs), which gives the leaf a grayish appearance.

The flowers are on a spike that rises above and from the center of the spirally arranged leaves to form a rosette. The tiny flowers are densely crowded and are perfect (have both male and female organs). Seeds are tiny and dark colored.

The common plantain (*Plantago major*) was probably brought to Hawai'i by early Chinese immigrants and became an important medicinal herb in Hawai'i. The Hawaiians soon adopted it as a substitute for their native *laukahi*, giving it the same name. *Laukahi* is widely distributed now and is considered a weed, especially in lawns and pathways.

This plantain is stemless, with leaves forming a rosette close to the ground. The shape and surface of the leaves differ from the native plantain in being broad-oval or almost heart-shaped, with leaf stems that are broad and troughed. The leaves are smooth on both surfaces. The margins are entire, the veins grooved, i.e., depressed, as seen from the upper surface.

The tiny flowers are borne in cylindrical heads at the upper end of long slender stalks. Fruiting capsules develop from the flowers and are very small; each capsule contains five to sixteen seeds. The capsules dehisce (they burst and the seeds scatter).

Medicinal Uses

Ancient

Thrush. *Laukahi* leaves were wrapped in ti leaves and broiled over embers. For young babies, the broiled *laukahi* leaves were chewed by the mother and then fed to the child. For children over two years old, increasing numbers of *laukahi* leaves were boiled, and these were fed directly to the child. However, for children older than one year, other formulations were preferred. The nursing mother also ate the *laukahi* leaves in order to pass on the medicine to the nursing child through her milk.

Boils. Leaves of *laukahi* were rubbed with salt until they were wilted, and then the salt was shaken off and the wilted leaves placed upon the boil. This application would be made in the morning and repeated again the next morning until the boil burst and the core and pus came to the surface. Sometimes a narrow piece of *kapa* of sufficient length was twisted, formed into a ring, and placed around the boil. The area within the *kapa* ring was then filled with the treated *laukahi* leaves, and the whole held in place with a *kapa* bandage. A variant of this treatment was to sprinkle salt on *laukahi* leaves and then to mash these and place the resulting mixture on the boil.

Wana (sea urchin) spine wounds. The crushed leaves of *laukahi* were applied to wounds made by *wana* to ease the pain and counteract the *wana* toxin.

Contemporary

Crushed or pounded *laukahi* leaves are still used as a

poultice for boils, using gauze bandages in place of strips of *kapa*.

Tea made from *laukahi* leaves (either fresh or dried) is used for diabetes.

Commercially, the seed husks of several other plantain are sold as a pharmaceutical product for constipation. These seeds are called "psyllium."

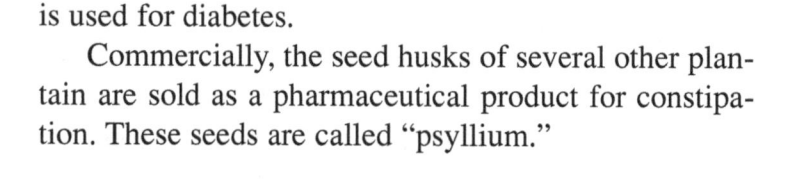

Limu kala

Hawaiian name: *Limu kala*
Common name: Seaweed
Scientific name: *Sargassum echinocarpum* J. Agardh

Limu are plants that grow in water, either fresh water (streams and ponds) or in salt water (the sea). The *limu* that grows in the sea is commonly called seaweed. Hawaiians used many *limu* of both kinds for medicine, but we are including only one in this book, *limu kala*.

 ## Description

A long, brown seaweed, *limu kala* has stems covered with short branches bearing stiff, twisted, more or less toothed leaves and small round floating bodies. The rough appearance of this *limu* gives it its name, *kala*, prickly or tough.

 ## Medicinal Uses

Ancient

Although many *limu* were eaten, *limu kala,* though edible, was seldom eaten because of its toughness. The chief use of *limu kala* as a medicine was symbolic. As a patient was recovering from an illness, an open-ended *lei* made from *limu kala* was draped around her (or his) neck and she walked into the ocean. As she walked out, the approaching waves would lift the *lei* from her neck, and as the *lei* was washed away, so also were the final symptoms of the disease washed away.

Thrush. For a child of from four to six weeks of age, a mixture of *limu kala, limu lipoa kai* (another seaweed favored because of its fragrance), and broiled *kalo* was chewed by the mother and transferred to the child's mouth.

❖ Contemporary

The symbolic use of *limu kala* is still important to many Hawaiian people. At the beach, if you step on coral, "snag" a length of floating *limu kala*, chew it, and place it on the wound.

Mai‘a

Hawaiian name: *Mai‘a*
Common name: Banana
Scientific name: *Musa* x *paradisiaca* L.

A number of varieties of *mai'a* were brought by the Polynesians when they came to Hawai'i from the Marquesas. These varieties were distinguished by suffixes that referred to plant characteristics; they will be noted later when describing their use in medicine. Today most of the bananas grown and found in the market are postcontact imports.

Description

In general, *mai'a* is a tall herb with a stalk (stem or "trunk") up to twenty feet tall, consisting of the bases of leaves (sheaths), which arise from an underground stem (corm). These leaf bases are arranged spirally and overlap. The leaf stems are thick, short to long, with the leaf blades large, fairly thick, and smooth and entire when they first unfurl but which split early along the parallel side veins to form a featherlike structure. The midrib is pronounced on the underside.

Flowers are borne in an inflorescence on a thick fruit stem that emerges from the top of the trunk (the center of the leaf blades cluster) and becomes pendent (hangs downward) in almost all varieties. The flowers are arranged in flat groups of two rows each, under large light to dark purplish red or green bracts. The male flowers occur at the fruit stem tip, the female flowers at the stem base. The bracts subtending (enclosing) the female and sterile flowers become dislodged and fall early, whereas those covering the male flowers persist to form a more or less tight "flower bud." The tepals (sepals and petals that are similar in appearance) of the female flower consist of one distinct (separate) and five fused parts forming a tube that appears to be split on one

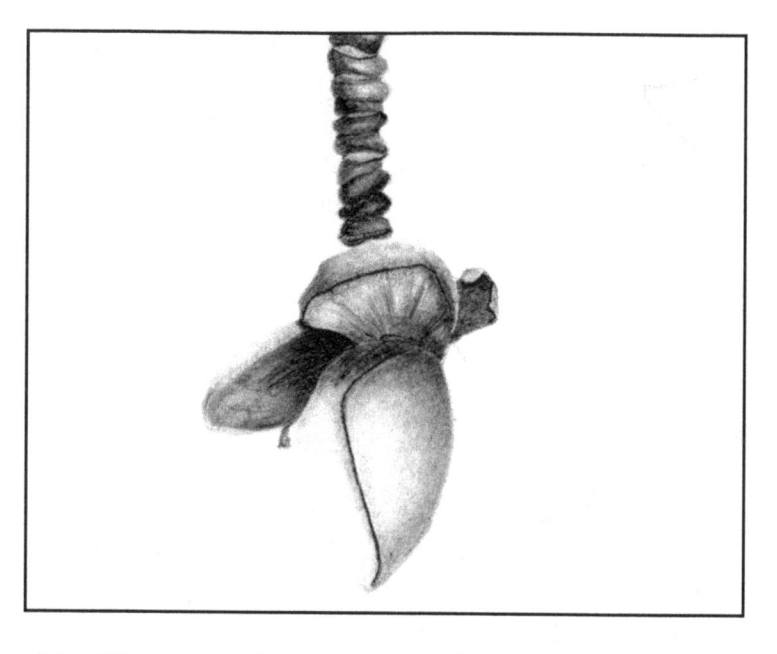

side. There are six stamens without anthers (pollen-bearing portions of the flower), and the inferior ovary is three-celled, with many ovules that do not develop into seeds in the varieties under consideration.

The fruits, which develop from the female flower at the base of the fruit stem, are long and cylindrical, with a skin that varies from yellow (the most common) to orange to red and covers an interior that is more or less fleshy and varies in color from cream to pink.

The individual fruits are commonly called "fingers"; they appear grouped in double rows, each group known as a "hand." A "bunch" is made up of a number of these hands. The fingers curve downward when the bunch is still on the stalk, and the bunch is cut down and hung by its stem. In commercial growing of bananas, the portion of the "bunch" stem on which the sterile and male flowers occur is cut off prior to harvest.

A stalk bears but a single bunch and thus is usually cut down at the time the bunch is harvested.

General Uses

The most important use of bananas for the ancient Hawaiians was of the fruit for food, as it is today. The Hawaiians divided the many banana varieties they grew or gathered from the wild into three classes: those eaten raw; those cooked in some manner before eating; and those that could be eaten either raw or cooked. All but three varieties were *kapu* (forbidden) to women.

 ## Medicinal Uses

 ### Ancient

It appears that, in general, specific varieties of bananas were used to treat specific diseases.

Thrush. At least five different varieties were used for the rather prevalent childhood disease known as *'ea* and for other childhood diseases. The varieties used were *mai'a 'ele'ele* (with a black trunk and orange-colored fruit flesh); *mai'a iho lena* (with a green trunk and purple, mottled-with-pink skin and salmon-pink fruit flesh); *mai'a lele* (with a yellowish green trunk, yellow-skinned fruit, and pink-colored fruit flesh; and *mai'a puapuanui* (which resembles the *mai'a iholena* and the *mai'a lele*, but which has plumper fruit).

Preparation of formulations using any one of these varieties was similar: the slimy sap from the cut flower bud and from the base of the trunk and corm (underground stem), which were chopped or crushed to make them "bleed," was mixed with sap from green (immature) *kukui* nuts. Other therapeutic elements, such as *'alaea*, were mixed in, and the concoction was then smeared on the tongue and lining of the mouth of the young patients.

A simpler formulation, using only sap from the cut end of the flower bud and suckers from the variety *mai'a iholena*, was mixed with the sap of green *kukui* nuts. This mixture was then applied to the child's mouth lining and tongue.

Asthma. For asthma, *pilali* (hardened gum from the *kukui* tree trunk) was left to stand overnight in a calabash filled with spring water. Young *'ihi mākole*, mature *noni* fruit, *'ōhi'a 'ai* bark, *kukui* flowers, dried *niu* flesh (broiled until crisp), *'ala'ala wai nui pehu*, rhizomes of *'ōlena*, *'alaea*, and *kō kea* were mixed and pounded and the liquid in the mash squeezed into a calabash. To this was added the liquid in which the *kukui* gum had soaked (the gum had to be pounded on a flat stone to make it dissolve). The mixed liquids were strained and placed in a large water gourd. Ashes obtained by burning dry banana (variety not specified) leaves and leaves of *mau'u pili hale* (probably *pili* grass) were added to the combined liquids. A mouthful of the medicine was drunk three times a day until all of it had been consumed. Food to be eaten while taking this medicine included two varieties of banana, *mai'a iho lena* and *mai'a lele*, cooked *lū'au*, fish, and unfermented *poi*. Tea made from *moa* was drunk in great quantities.

Constipation. The flesh of ripe *mai'a koa'e* fruit was scraped and left to stand in a calabash. To this was added the grated flesh of the *lauloa* variety of *kalo* and the chewed kernels of green *kukui* nuts. The slimy sap from the inner bark of *hau* branches was placed in another calabash along with chewed *kukui* flowers and leaf buds and fresh spring water. The contents of this second calabash were mixed and pounded to a mash, and the liquid strained from this mixture was added to the contents of the first calabash. The whole was mixed and squeezed and strained and the liquid heated with hot stones. The cooled medicine was taken in the morning.

Heartburn. Ashes obtained by burning the dried leaves of *mai'a 'ele'ele* were shaken on a daub of *poi kalo* and eaten with a drink of fresh spring water for relief of heartburn.

Listlessness. A tonic was made to treat listlessness. Sometimes the end of the flower bud of banana was nipped to obtain drops of sap. The sap was given to babies and young children who seemed listless. The sap is rich in vitamins, so this ancient medicine may be considered analogous to the cod liver oil once given to Western babies and young children with the same symptoms.

Tuberculosis. The corm of a young shoot of the banana variety known as *mai'a pōpō'ulu* was pounded and mixed with the bark of the taproots of *'uhaloa* and *puakala* (native prickly white poppy, *Argemone glauca*); bark of a branch of *'ōhi'a 'ai* and the *kukui* tree trunk; *kohekohe*; *pōpolo* berries, leaf buds, and leaves; and *kō kea*. All these ingredients were mixed together and pounded to a mash, and the concoction was squeezed to obtain a liquid that was heated with hot stones. When cool, the liquid was taken as a drink in the evenings for five days.

Chest pains. The sap from the cut-off stalk of an unidentified banana variety was added to the slimy sap from the inner bark of *hau*. Powdered *'alaea* was added and all the ingredients mixed together. *Kō kea* was chewed and the juice dripped into the above-mentioned mixture. The flesh and slimy sap of leaf shoots from *kikawaiō* were chewed and spat into the mixture and strained. The clear liquid was divided into two equal parts: one to be taken in the morning; the other, at night. Teas made from *ko'oko'olau* and *moa* were frequently drunk in combination with this medicine.

Contemporary

Drops of sap obtained by nipping off the tip of a flower bud are still used as a source of vitamins, especially for children.

The broiled flesh of green banana fruits is prescribed for the control of diarrhea.

Māmaki

Hawaiian name: *Māmaki*
Scientific name: *Pipturus* spp.

Māmaki, often misspelled *māmake,* is a native (endemic) plant with several species. Some of these species are limited to certain areas on several of the Hawaiian islands or to one island only. The "convenient" species was used, since all species had the features that made this genus valuable. A member of the nettle family, this plant is usually found on the outskirts of forests at mid-altitude.

The following description covers the general and specific characteristics of the genus.

Description

Māmaki is a small shrub or tree that grows up to fifteen feet in height. The stem and branches have a smooth, light-brown bark and watery sap. Young branches are covered with a mat of gray, woolly hairs.

Leaves are usually thin and have reddish veins, which are usually raised. The leaf margins are usually serrated. The petioles are long, and stipules (leaflike bracts at the base of the petiole) are present. The underside of the leaf appears grayish, due to the presence of a mat of woolly hairs. The leaves are arranged alternately on the stem.

Flowers are unisexual (with either male or female sexual organs but not both); both male and female flowers may be borne on the same plant or on separate plants. The female flowers are sessile (attached directly at their base to the branch), in headlike clusters in the axils of petioles. Male flowers also occur in similar headlike clusters.

Fruit formed from the female flower is usually covered with coarse hairs and varies in color from gray to pale yellow to pale-to-yellowish brown.

General Uses

Kapa was beaten from the fibrous inner bark, and cordage was made from the isolated fibers.

 ## Medicinal Uses

Ancient

Thrush. This use of preventive medicine to control the childhood disease known as *'ea* is different from all others presented in this book in that medication began with the pregnant mother.

When the mother was five months pregnant, she ate five *māmaki* fruit and continued until she was eight or nine months pregnant, when she ate eight fruits. After the child was born, the mother, after chewing the fruit to soften it, gave two fruits to the baby until he (or she) was four months old. Once the child could consume (chew and swallow) on his own, he ate six or eight fruits until he was a year old.

Listlessness. Tea made from fresh leaves, placed in a gourd calabash to which fresh spring water and red-hot stones were added, was drunk as a tonic for what in old-fashioned terminology was called "general debility" (a feeling of weakness or just a "blah" feeling). Hot water is therapeutic in itself and thus enhanced the active element in the *māmaki* leaf.

◈ Contemporary

As popular as tea made from *koʻokoʻolau* leaves was and still is, tea made from *māmaki* leaves is almost, if not even more widely used today, not only as a tonic but also for various illnesses. Health food stores sell packaged dried *māmaki* leaves, labeled *māmaki* tea. It has a more pleasing aroma and taste than *koʻokoʻolau* tea, which may explain its popularity.

Niu

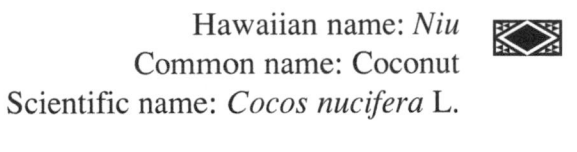

Hawaiian name: *Niu*
Common name: Coconut
Scientific name: *Cocos nucifera* L.

The *niu* tree is primarily a strand plant, growing near the sea. Since the ripe fruit is buoyant, it may travel some distances by floating along the shore of an island or even between islands to plant itself. However, a *niu* could not have remained viable long enough to have floated from other Pacific islands to Hawai'i.

Niu is of great importance to the Polynesians, including the Marquesans, who brought it to Hawai'i.

Niu derives its scientific name *Cocos* from the Portuguese word *coco*, meaning monkey, referring to the resemblance of the *niu* to a monkey's face because of the three holes at the end of the nut.

Description

The *niu* dominant in Hawai'i is a very tall tree with a comparatively slender trunk, thicker at the base. A mature tree can reach a height of one hundred feet and live up to one hundred years.

The leaves (fronds) are clustered, like a feather duster, at the top of the trunk. They are large, from six to eighteen feet long and two to six feet wide, and lie flat. The frond stems are long, smooth, and comparatively thick, with fibrous, trunk-clasping bases. Encasing these bases are fibrous, fabriclike sheaths. Numerous leaflets, in two rows, one on each side of the stem, are from one to three feet long.

A tree may begin to flower when it is only six years old. Both sexes are found in the same simple clusters, which occur among the fronds. The small, cream-colored male flowers are borne in great numbers on long branches, while the female flowers, considerably larger and fewer in number, are located at the bases of the branches.

The fruit, a nut, ripens in nine to ten months. In general shape, it may be almost round or somewhat elongated, six to twelve inches long. A cross section through the entire fruit would be more or less triangular. The "skin" or "shell" is yellowish to orange when immature, and grayish when ripe. This skin covers a thick, fibrous husk, which in turn covers the hard, fairly thin shell of the nut. Inside the shell is a layer of white, solid, edible sweet pulp, popularly called "flesh" or "meat," surrounding a hollow filled with a more or less clear, sweet liquid called "water." The *niu* is propagated by planting the fruit (the entire nut with husk).

 General Uses

The *niu* was a very important plant to the ancient Hawaiians. They used the fronds for thatching the roofs of canoe sheds; the heavy bases of the frond stems to pound the banks of their *lo'i*; the base of the trunk for temple drums; the fibers in the husks of the fruit for cordage—one of the most important uses; the shells of the nuts for utensils; the water in the nut for drinking on long voyages; the meat to extract oil for their bodies; and after a migration from Tahiti, the "cream" squeezed from grated meat in cooking.

Medicinal Uses

Ancient

Probably the most important use of *niu* in the practice of herbal medicine was as material for squeezing the juice (sap) from mashed plant material. The fibrous, fabriclike sheath at the base of young *niu* leaves is light-colored and pliable. It is, however, covered on both sides with debris, which was scraped off to leave a material much resembling cheesecloth. Today, this material is frequently used for the same purpose, i.e., to squeeze juice from a macerated pulp.

Both the *niu* flesh and the water were used in formulations. Examples of such use are given below.

Asthma ("stubborn case"). Eight *'ākia* (fish poison plant, *Wikstroemia* spp.) leaves were added to a man's hatful (a postcontact measurement) of *naio* leaf buds and leaves; two pieces (no size indicated) of *'ōhi'a* (probably *'ōhi'a 'ai*) bark; the bark of four *'uhaloa* roots; one-half the dried flesh of a mature *niu*; and one long section of *kō kea*. These were pounded together to a mash, mixed, squeezed, strained in the usual manner, and cooled. The patient drank the mixture while lying face down. Five doses (size of dose not indicated) were taken both morning and evening, for five days.

Bladder trouble (urine retention). A handful of the

bracts from the bases of stems of the native sedge *makaloa* (*Cyperus laevigatus*, from which beautiful sleep mats were made); a slice from each of three forms of *'awa*: *'awa hiwa*, *'awa mō'i*, and *'awa papa*, the size of a fist; the whitish part of light ti leaf buds; and one "root" (rhizome) of *'ōlena* the size of a *kukui* nut, along with lumps of *'alaea* and gray *pālolo* (clay) the size of a *kukui* nut, were pounded to a mash and mixed. Then three-fourths cup of "water" from a young *niu* fruit was added and the concoction squeezed out and strained in the usual manner. Small hot stones were added to the liquid and the medicine drunk twice a day until five doses had been drunk. Much fresh spring water and *ko'oko'olau* tea was drunk during the period of medication.

Contemporary

There appears to be little use of *niu* by practitioners or others today. One report of the use of *niu* water for kidney "trouble" was found in the literature.

Noni

Hawaiian name: *Noni*
Common name: Indian mulberry
Scientific name: *Morinda citrifolia* L.

Noni, Morinda citrifolia, received its genus name, *Morinda*, from the Latin words *morus* (mulberry) and *indicus* (Indian), referring to its fruit, which resembles that of the Indian or true mulberry; and its species name, *citrifolia*, from the shape of its leaves (*folia*), which is like those of citrus (*citri*).

Noni is a native tree, brought to Hawai'i by the original Polynesian settlers who came to Hawai'i from the Marquesas.

The tree has become naturalized in both dry and somewhat moister open areas and in dry and moister forests.

 Description

Noni is a small evergreen tree or, in adverse growing conditions, a shrub. It is from nine to eighteen feet or more in height. The branches are angular, and the branchlets thick and marked with leaf scars. The leaves are conspicuous, large (eight to sixteen inches wide), somewhat ovate (oval) to elliptical in shape, glossy, dark green, and deeply veined, with short, stout petioles.

Flowers form in globe-shaped "heads," each of which is up to four or more inches long. These "heads" bear many flowers, which open one or two at a time, until all the flowers have bloomed. The individual flowers are small and tubular, with a white five-lobed corolla.

The "head" bearing the flower increases slowly in size during the blooming period and more rapidly when flowering has been completed. The fruit is a fleshy syncarp ("head"), which when mature is somewhat warty, with a thin yellowish white "skin" marked with polygonal pitted figures, the bases of the flowers. The flesh of the mature fruit is solid and white. The flesh of the ripe (often referred to as "overripe") fruit is soft and fetid (very foul-smelling). A unique feature of the seed is an attached air chamber.

 General Uses

In ancient Hawai'i, *noni* was primarily used to colorize *kapa*, with a red dye in the inner bark of the trunk and a yellow dye in the inner bark of the root. The mature fruit became a famine food; it is edible but not very palatable.

Medicinal Uses

Ancient

Boils. In early days, and somewhat into the present day, the flesh of the ripe *noni* fruit (probably with the seeds removed) was mashed and applied to boils as a poultice. In early times a narrow strip of *kapa* was twisted and placed in a circle around the affected area to make an enclosure for the mashed fruit. Another wider strip of *kapa* was used to keep the *noni* pulp and its enclosure in place. Today, a gauze bandage is used in place of *kapa*.

Constipation. Mature and ripe fruit was added to various formulations in which other plant products played more important roles. For example, *noni* was sometimes added to an enema consisting of the sap from the inner bark of the *hau* stem for constipation.

As a tonic. It has also been reported that *noni* leaves

were brewed for a tea. Made from either fresh or dried leaves, this tea was drunk as a kind of tonic.

Deep cuts and compound fractures. The unripe fruit was pounded and the resulting mash was applied to deep cuts and compound fractures.

▨ Contemporary

There has been a recent (since 1996) surge of interest in the medicinal uses of *noni*, especially for the treatment of internal ills. Today, *noni* continues to be used as a poultice. *Noni* leaves, either green or dried, are sometimes used to make a tea to drink as a tonic or "cleansing" agent. *Noni* leaves wilted over a flame are sometimes taped over cysts or growths on the skin and allowed to remain overnight; *noni* pulp is also sometimes used for the same purpose. Made into a salve, the fruit pulp is used to get rid of head lice. Some people use the sap from *noni* to treat kidney problems, high blood pressure, diabetes, and bowel problems, as well as some kinds of cancers.

An ingenious method of obtaining the sap, which is the ingredient of the plant most often used, is to place the ripe (so-called "overripe") fruit in large, closed, clear-glass jars, which are placed in the sun. The heat of the sun causes the fruit to ferment and release a "clear" sap. This is certainly an easier and quicker method of getting the liquid from the fruit than the old Hawaiian way, which was to pound the fruit to a mash and then squeeze out the liquid and strain it.

There is at least one present-day practitioner, who gathers Hawaiian medicinal herbs in high-altitude forests, who does not use *noni*. In fact, this practitioner believes that *noni* is actually either harmful or useless. But other practitioners who use *noni* explain that herbalists gather medicine from the places they know: upland dwellers gather upland herbs; lowland dwellers gather lowland herbs. And *noni* is a lowland herb.

Because of the popularity of *noni* as a medicine, the demand for the fruit has grown dramatically. *Noni* trees in residential private gardens have been stripped of their fruits, both green and ripe. In normal circumstances the trees would be loaded with fruits at all stages of development, with many ripe fruits lying on the ground near the base of the tree.

The fruit has been for sale in at least one supermarket, where it was marked at eight dollars per pound. Even a *noni* pill appeared in at least one health food store, but the State Department of Health banned its sale, and rightly so, because after "processing," *noni* fruit or sap retains few or no medicinal properties.

'Ōhi'a 'ai

Hawaiian name: *'Ōhi'a 'ai*
Common name: Mountain apple or Malay apple
Scientific name: *Syzygium malaccense* (L.) Merr. and Perry

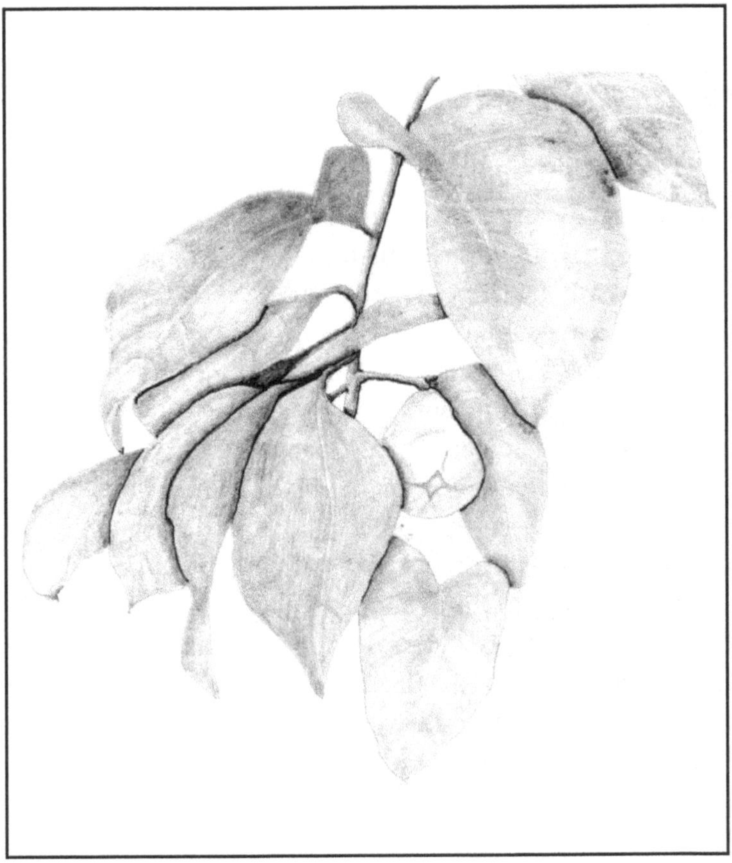

'Ōhi'a 'ai was brought to Hawai'i by the first settlers, who came from the Marquesas. It was usually planted in shady valleys and eventually formed groves.

After contact, people planted individual *'ōhi'a 'ai* trees in their yards or private gardens, but that is not so common now.

The *'ōhi'a 'ai* belongs to the myrtle family, to which *kuawa* also belongs.

Description

'Ōhi'a 'ai is a handsome tree, reaching heights of fifty feet or less when growing naturally in groves in shady valleys. Growing alone, this tree may become shrubby.

The bark is smooth and gray, somewhat mottled. The oval leaves are dark green and shiny.

The trees bloom in March or April, with the individual flowers growing out on short stems from the trunk and branches. The cerise flowers are tassellike (forming pompoms); the cerise color is that of the stamens.

The fruit, about three inches long and two inches in diameter, consists of a crisp, pure-white, juicy flesh, surrounded by a thin, deep-crimson skin. The flesh tastes slightly sweet and is very refreshing. A single large seed is embedded in the flesh.

There is a white-flowered, white-fruited form of *'ōhi'a 'ai* that bears no seed.

 General Uses

Eating large quantities of the fruit causes diarrhea. Drying the fruit, a practice of ancient Hawaiians, eliminates this disadvantage.

Medicinal Uses
Ancient

Thrush and other children's diseases. Bark from branches of *'ōhi'a 'ai, 'ōhi'a lehua liko* (young leaves); *kukui* flowers; leaves and leaf buds of *hinahina kū kahakai* (a creeping form of heliotrope, *Heliotropium anomalum*); buds of *'aka'akai 'oliana* (a species of *Allium*, or onion; because the suffix *'oliana* is a Hawaiianization of "oleander," it is clear that this plant was a postcontact addition; NOTE: *'aka'akai 'oliana* is a kind of onion, not the poisonous ornamental shrub oleander); *'uhaloa* flowers, leaf buds and some older leaves; and sugarcane (*honua'ula* variety, with a red rind) were mixed together and pounded to a mash. The liquid in this mash was squeezed out in the usual manner and strained. The strained liquid was given to children, the child's age determining the amount of medicine. Younger children were given the medicine twice a day, and older children, three times a day.

Deep cuts and open wounds. The bark of branches of *'ōhi'a 'ai* was mixed with salt and the two were pounded together into a mash. The mash was squeezed and the liquid thus obtained was poured into the wound. Those treated were warned that the burning sensation must be endured, as it was the healing agent.

Bad breath with white coating on the tongue. A combination of *'ōhi'a 'ai* bark, *moa*, and *kō kea* were mixed, pounded, and placed in a gourd calabash. Spring water was added, and the whole was mixed thoroughly. The liquid was squeezed out, strained, and placed in a large water gourd. A mouthful was gargled each morning, at noon, and in the evening for five days. A small amount of the medicine was drunk after each gargling.

Ko'oko'olau tea was frequently drunk during the "cure" period.

Sore throat. A piece of *'ōhi'a 'ai* bark was chewed for sore throat.

 ## Contemporary

Pieces of bark from younger branches are still chewed for sore throats. The macerated plant tissue can be swallowed with the sap that has been released in chewing or it can be spat out.

ʻŌhiʻa lehua

Hawaiian name: *ʻŌhiʻa lehua* (often shortened to *ʻōhiʻa* or *lehua*)
Scientific name: *Metrosideros polymorpha* Gaud.

'Ōhi'a lehua is a native (endemic) tree dearly beloved by Hawaiians and others because of both its beauty and its usefulness.

'Ōhi'a lehua belongs to the myrtle family, the same family as guava and eucalyptus. Its genus name, *Metrosideros,* is Greek for "heart of iron," referring in this case to its hard wood. The species name, *polymorpha*, points out the many forms (great variation) of this plant; these forms will be enumerated in the description of this plant.

At one time, *'ōhi'a lehua* grew in great forests on the slopes of Mauna Kea and Mauna Loa on the island of Hawai'i; some trees grew as tall as one hundred feet. Some of these trees can still be found there. Younger trees are found on lava flows, where *'ōhi'a lehua* is often the first plant, after mosses and ferns, to grow on the cooling lava. Isolated trees or small groves of *'ōhi'a lehua* are found on all the larger islands.

 ## Description

Botanists recognize eight varieties of *Metrosideros polymorpha*, differentiated by the size of the plant, the type of bark, the shapes and characters of leaves, and the natural habitat (island and elevation). Hawaiians also indicated different varieties by adding a suffix, as in *'ōhi'a kea* (or *lehua kea*), the white-flowered variety, and *'ōhi'a lau li'i* (or *lehua lau li'i*), the *'ōhi'a lehua* with very small leaves.

'Ōhi'a lehua may take the form of a tall, erect tree or a medium-sized gnarled shrub. The bark may be rough and fissured (cracked) or smooth and, in either case, in older trees may flake off.

There is a great variety in the shape and character of

leaves, from round to elongated, thin or thick, tips pointed or rounded, sometimes with smooth surfaces on both sides of the leaf but more frequently "woolly" on the underside.

Flowers appear in clusters and are perfect (have all parts, both female and male). The sepals and petals are inconspicuous; the stamens are the showy part of the flower and give the flower a pompom appearance. The stamens are most frequently red (all shades) but may also be orange, pink, yellow, or, rarely, white.

The fruit is a capsule that contains tiny seeds. In a mixed *'ōhi'a lehua/hāpu'u* forest, *hāpu'u* serves as a kind of "nursery" for these tiny seeds, which fall on them.

 ## General Uses

In ancient Hawai'i, the red-flowered *'ōhi'a lehua* was dedicated to Pele, the goddess of volcanoes. The flower was the subject of many legends and songs. The flowers, capsules and *leko* (young, usually colored leaves) were used for *lei*. The wood was used in some types of construction and for making idols, spears, and mallets.

Today, the wood is greatly prized for hardwood flooring, furniture, carvings, and other items made generally from hard woods.

 ## Medicinal Uses

Ancient

No particular variety of this plant seems to have been preferred for medicines. Use may have depended upon availability.

Childbirth pains. Four flower clusters of *'ōhi'a lehua* and a strip of the inner bark of *hau* the length of a man's arm were used for this medicine. The slimy *hau* bark was scraped into a *niu*-shell bowl, and fresh spring water was added. These two ingredients were mixed, the *'ōhi'a lehua* flowers were added, and all were hand mixed. This mixture was then squeezed and the resulting liquid strained in the usual manner. This medicine was given to the woman in labor when the pains of childbirth became intense.

Thrush. One man's hatful (modern measurement) of *'ōhi'a lehua* (sometimes a mixture of several varieties) *leko*, and one man's hatful (modern measurement) *lama* leaves, leaf buds, and flowers were pounded together in a bowl. One small long-necked water gourd full of fresh spring water was added, and the mixture was left overnight. The next morning four red-hot stones were added. When the concoction had cooled, the liquid was squeezed out and strained in the usual manner. The child was given this drink along with *poi lehua*, made from *kalo lehua*, a taro with pinkish corm flesh and stems. In addition, much *ko'oko'olau* tea was given to drink.

▧ Contemporary

Flowers are still given to mothers in labor to alleviate birthing pains.

ʻŌlena

Hawaiian name: *ʻŌlena*
Common name: Turmeric
Scientific name: *Curcuma longa* L.

'Ōlena, a member of the ginger family, is known else-where as turmeric, a spice that is an ingredient of curry powder. 'Ōlena was brought to Hawai'i by the Marquesans, the earliest settlers.

 ## Description

'Ōlena is stemless, with several leaves that arise direct-ly from thick rhizomes. The leaves form a cluster, twen-ty inches or more high. The leaves come up in the spring and die back in the fall. They are light green, thin, and eight inches long and three inches wide or larger. Petioles are as long as the leaf blades or longer and overlap to form a false stem.

The inflorescence forms a cylindrical "head" about five inches long. The head is borne on a long stem, which emerges from the center of the leaves, each of which subtends (covers) two or more small pale yellow flowers, except at the top of the head, where the bracts are pink and where there are no flowers. Seeds are rare.

Externally, rhizomes of 'ōlena look much like those of culinary ginger, but whereas the interior of culinary ginger is white, the interior of 'ōlena is colored in a range of yellows and yellow-oranges. A young 'ōlena rhizome is yellow, and as it matures the color changes to orange, then gold, and finally to mustard.

 ## General Uses

In ancient Hawai'i the rhizomes were an important source of dye for *kapa*. Although throughout Southeast

Asia and other parts of the world turmeric is used as a spice, it was not used as such in precontact Hawai'i.

 ## Medicinal Uses

Ancient

Stuffy nose, sinus troubles. Rhizomes of '*ōlena*, '*awapuhi kuahiwi*, '*awapuhi lei* (a postcontact introduced ornamental ginger), '*awapuhi kuahiwi* flower buds, and *kō kea* were pounded together. The resulting mix was squeezed into a *niu*-shell "cup." Into this cup was squeezed the sudsy sap obtained by squeezing a head of '*awapuhi kuahiwi*. The two liquids were thoroughly mixed. The final liquid was dripped onto a ball of *hāpu'u*, which was then wrapped in a piece of *kapa*. The patient inhaled the "fumes" from this medicated ball five to ten times a day until the affliction disappeared. A fresh preparation was made each day.

Evidently, the above-described treatment was accompanied by gargling with a liquid made by pounded-together pieces of bark from *kukui* and '*ōhi'a 'ai* trunks with *kukui* flowers and leaves of *moa holokula*. The liquid squeezed from the concoction was thoroughly mixed, "water" from a *niu* was added, and the whole used as a gargle twice a day, morning and evening, for four days.

Along with the gargling, a liquid made of the same ingredients as the gargle but without the *niu* "water," and with the addition of burnt *kī*, mature *noni* fruit, and *niu* meat was taken as a drink three times each day: morning, noon, and night.

Blood purifier. To "purify" the blood (which could

mean a treatment for a multitude of ills), a liquid was made by squeezing out a mash made by pounding together *'ōlena* rhizomes; leaf buds, leaves, and taproots of *pāwale* (a native dock, *Rumex giganteus*); and trunk barks from *koa* and *'ōhia 'ai,* with some juice from *kō kea*. This medicine was taken as a drink twice a day.

It is also reported that a liquid obtained by pounding the *'ōlena* rhizomes was used for earache. No record of the preparation of a formulation for this use was found in literature.

Contemporary

Today, a liquid obtained by macerating the *'ōlena* rhizome and squeezing it through cheesecloth is introduced into the nostrils as a remedy for sinus problems. It would be safer to pour the liquid on some absorbent material and inhale the "fumes" as the ancient Hawaiians did.

There are also reports of a similar application into the ear for earache.

Panini O'awa'awa

Hawaiian name: *Panini 'awa'awa*
Common name: Aloe
Scientific name: *Aloe vera* (L.) N.L. Burm.

Panini ʻawaʻawa is the older Hawaiian name for this plant. The first word, *panini*, refers to its cactuslike appearance, and *ʻawaʻawa* to the "sour," acid taste of its sap. Today the plant is more commonly called aloe, pronounced "aloy" in Hawaiʻi instead of "alow," as in the scientific name and in general usage outside Hawaiʻi.

Aloe belongs to the group of plants known as "xerophytes," plants that lose water very slowly because they possess a viscous sap and, usually, a thick epidermis, or "skin." They are also called "succulents." Such plants are adapted to grow in hot, dry areas.

Aloe is a postcontact introduction. Although this book is concerned primarily with precontact medicinal plants, aloe is included because it was adopted by Hawaiians and other ethnic groups for medicinal use very soon after its introduction into Hawaiʻi. In fact, many people in Hawaiʻi consider aloe a native plant.

 Description

Aloe is a short-stemmed plant with thick, sword-shaped leaves crowded together to form a rosette. With age, the stem elongates and the plant loses its rosette-like appearance, forming a low, "landy" shrub.

The leaves vary in coloration and marking; they are either solid light green or light green with white spots. The margins also vary; they are either smooth or have "soft" spines. The leaf interior contains a clear, viscous sap.

A cluster of flowers is borne at the end of a tall stem arising from the center of the rosette, or at the top of the elongated stem. Individual flowers are narrowly tubular, spreading slightly at the throat. They are red or yellow, depending on the variety.

General Uses

Because of its xerophytic character, aloe is used in landscaping in areas where the rainfall is low and irrigation at a premium.

 Medicinal Uses

Burns. Older texts on Hawaiian medicinal herbs do not refer to this plant, because it was a postcontact introduction. The primary use for many years after its introduction was as a treatment for burns. Whether this was the first or only use after the plant's arrival in Hawai'i I do not know, but I do remember its being used for burns when I was a child, some ninety years ago.

Long-time residents and many later arrivals have a pot of aloe on their kitchen stoop or back stairs. Since probably the largest number of burns occur in the kitchen, it is convenient to have this medicinal plant at hand.

The plant is ideally suited for the treatment of burns. First of all, the viscous sap, a semiliquid, is easy to apply in a thin layer over the affected area, where it quickly dries to form an airtight covering over the burn. "Cutting off" the air relieves the pain and prevents infection. Also, the sap contains tannin, the primary ingredient of commercial burn ointments, and other healing elements such as antibiotics.

The leaf is usually cut across its width and the exposed surface, oozing with sap, is rubbed on the burned surface. Additional cuts of the leaf are made to expose fresh "sappy" tissue for additional applications.

Another method of application was and is to remove

(cut away) the dense rigid "skin" (external tissue) on both sides of the leaf and lay the exposed "sappy" slab of tissue on the burn. In the early days, this "slab" was tied on with a band of *kapa*. Today, it is tied on with a gauze bandage. This slab is replaced with a fresh one when needed.

Scars. Slabs of aloe inner tissue or sap from leaves is placed on scars to hasten their fading.

The sap from an aloe leaf is effectively used externally for sunburn, insect bites, rashes, and chapped lips. At one time, a Maui resident grew an acreage of aloe from which he prepared a solution he bottled and gave to friends and interested persons, primarily for chapped lips.

High blood pressure, stomach ulcers, diabetes. In recent years, gallon bottles of an aloe solution have been for sale in Hawai'i for internal use, prescribed for such diseases as hypertension (high blood pressure), stomach ulcers, diabetes, and cancer. This product is prepared by a grower in Texas and is sold in "beauty parlors" in Honolulu for $39.99. This is a ridiculously high price to pay for a product that could be prepared at home from a garden plant costing less than twenty-five cents! The home product could be made more palatable by using orange juice as the "base" instead of water, at the same time enhancing this "medicine" with vitamin C.

Pōhuehue

Hawaiian name: *Pōhuehue*
Common name: Beach morning glory
Scientific name: *Ipomoea pes-caprae* (L.) R. Br.

Pōhuehue belongs to the morning glory family, as its common name indicates. It is a native (indigenous) plant. The subspecies *brasiliensis* occurs in Hawai'i.

The genus name *Ipomoea* comes from the Greek words *ips*, worm, and *homoios*, wormlike, referring to the twining habit of the plant. The species name describes the shape of the leaf, which resembles the hoofprint (*pes*) of a goat (*caprae*).

 Description

Pōhuehue is a vigorously growing hardy vine found along sandy beaches above the high-water mark. The runners, or stems, up to fifteen feet long, grow from a thickened taproot. The stems are fleshy when young but become woody with age; secondary roots form at the nodes.

The leaves are roundish, but broader than long, smooth, fleshy, light green, and notched at the tip, having, as already noted, the appearance of a goat's hoofprint. The leaf blade is usually half-folded along the midrib (vein).

The flower, which usually occurs singly, is bell-shaped and a dusty pink. Most of the flowers are open in the morning, hence the common name "morning glory."

The fruit is a small, smooth capsule containing about four dark brown downy (hairy) seeds.

General Uses

In old Hawai'i, the roots and stems were eaten in times

of famine but with caution, i.e., in small amounts, since the plant can be poisonous.

The vines were slapped on the surface of the ocean, inside an encircling net, to drive fish into the net. The surface of the ocean was also whipped with strands of the vine to create waves for surfing.

Medicinal Uses

Ancient

Cleaning the blood. The following were mixed together and pounded to a mash: four *pōhuehue* taproots; eight pieces of *koki'o* (a native hibiscus) taproot; four pieces of *'ahakea* bark the size of an open hand; the bark of eight *'uhaloa* taproots; the stalk of one *kikānia* plant, with leaves, leaf buds, flowers, and taproot, but not the burs; the inner fleshy part of two *hāpu'u* trunks, half dried; two *'auko'i* stalks; four large mature *noni* fruit; and one and one-half sections of the sugarcane variety *kō honua'ula*. This macerated mixture was placed in a gourd calabash, and a water gourd full of fresh spring water was added. Two red-hot stones were placed in the covered calabash to "cook" the mixture. When this mixture had cooled, the stones were removed, and the juice was squeezed from the concoction in the usual manner. The juice was allowed to stand in the bowl for a period, then strained as usual, and placed in a long-necked gourd similar to a water gourd. One mouthful of this medicine was drunk three times a day, before eating. Large quantities of *ko'oko'olau* tea were drunk during the period of medication.

Lung trouble ("consumption") with high fever. The

bark of four taproots of *pōhuehue*; two men's hatfuls (postcontact measurement) of the stems, leaves and roots of *hinahina* (native heliotrope); and three handfuls of the ashes obtained by burning dried *naio* were mixed and pounded. To this macerated mixture were added two to three small long-necked water gourds full of fresh spring water and the whole mixed in a gourd calabash. Eight red-hot stones were added to the concoction. The patient, wearing a head covering, inhaled the resulting steam. This process was repeated each morning for five days. The patient received a special diet during the period of medication and was kept quiet and resting. He or she was given a dosage of *koali 'awa* when the medication period was over.

Sprains. A quantity of crushed *pōhuehue* leaves were mixed with salt and placed as a dressing on a sprain.

Contemporary

A poultice of crushed *pōhuehue* leaves, with or without salt, is still often used today for sprains.

Pōpolo

Hawaiian name: *Pōpolo*
Common name: Glossy nightshade
Scientific name: *Solanum americanum* Mill.

Although *pōpolo* was first collected in Hawai'i in 1835, after the arrival of Westerners, it is believed to be a native (indigenous) plant because seeds were found in the ancient Mauna Kea adze, which had been abandoned before Cook's arrival in 1778. It may, of course, have been brought by the Polynesians who settled in Hawai'i, since it is widely distributed in other tropical areas.

 Description

Pōpolo is an annual or a short-lived perennial shrublike herb three feet or more tall; it may be fairly erect and thin, spreading and even straggling when old. Leaves are thin, smooth, and about four inches long on new growth. They are simple and arranged alternately on the stem. They are ovate-lanceolate (egg-shaped, longer than wide, with a tapering tip). The margins are usually entire or shallowly lobed. Winglike bracts occur at the junction of petioles, which are relatively short, and stem.

Flowers, three to ten in number, are perfect (have both sexes) and occur in pendent clusters and at the tip of pedicels ("branches") about an inch long. They are small and white or lavender-tinted. The fruits, which have numerous tiny seeds, are glossy black berries, juicy and edible. They drop when ripe.

Pōpolo grows in Hawai'i in open areas from coastal regions to wet forests.

General Uses

The berries were reportedly used for a purple dye, and

the leaves for a green dye, but I doubt it. The ancient Hawaiians probably ate the berry, since it is palatable.

Westerners used the berries as a substitute for blueberries. I remember going out with a pail on Saturday mornings to collect a pailful of berries for my mother. The pail soon filled, since *pōpolo* is a widespread, heavy-bearing shrub. My mother used the berries to make jam and as a filling for pies and in muffins.

Medicinal Uses

Ancient

In old Hawai'i, it was said; "*O ka pōpolo ke kumu o ka lapa'au o Hawai'i nei*," referring to the belief that *pōpolo* is the foundation of Hawaiian pharmacy. *Pōpolo* was considered one of the visible forms of the great god Kāne and as such was referred to as Kāne-*pōpolo*.

Asthma. The bark of twelve large *pōpolo* taproots; one *niu*-shell cupful of the flowers, leaf buds, and four older leaves from *pōpolo* plants; the flesh of half a mature *niu*; four mature *noni* fruit; and two sections of *kō kea* were all mixed and pounded into a mash. Liquid was squeezed from this mixture, strained, and placed in a gourd calabash. Two small red-hot stones were placed in the calabash to cook the liquid; when the liquid was cooked and cooled, it was ready for drinking. The entire *'apu* was drunk at one time with the patient lying face down. Then the patient was given some dried *mai'a* fruit of the varieties *iho lena* and *maoli*, with an "after drink" of water from a mature *niu*. Five such medicinal *'apu* were drunk in the morning and five in the evening.

Abdominal trouble, possibly appendicitis. The bark of eight *pōpolo* taproots; two pieces of *'ō'hia 'ai* (mountain apple bark); and two sections of *kō kea* were mixed and pounded to a mash and placed in a gourd calabash. Separately, a *niu* cup packed full of the seaweed *limu 'ele'ele kai* (*Enteromorpha prolifera*) was mixed with a *niu*-shell cupful of fresh spring water. Then the one mixture was added to the other and the whole cooked by adding "four and two" (six) red-hot stones to the calabash. When the mixture had cooled, the stones were removed, the concoction was squeezed, and the resulting liquid left to stand for a while and then strained in the usual manner. A mouthful of the medicine was taken in the morning and again at night, for five days. *Ko'oko'olau* tea was drunk constantly during the period of medication, and a purgative administered after the final dose.

Contemporary

The raw sap from leaves and the juice from berries of *pōpolo* are used for all disorders of the respiratory tract.

Crushed leaves are mixed with salt to heal cuts and other wounds.

As an aid to digestion, the tender young leaves at the tips of branches are steeped with a little salt and eaten.

To cure a cold, steam *pōpolo* leaves that have been wrapped in *kī* leaves. Remove *pōpolo* leaves, divide into five equal portions, and eat one portion in the evening for five consecutive days.

For indigestion, rub a handful of *pōpolo* leaves on your *'ōpū* (stomach).

ʻUala

Hawaiian name: *ʻUala* or *ʻuwala*
Common name: Sweet potato
Scientific name: *Ipomoea batatas* (L.) Lam.

'Uala was brought to Hawai'i by the original settlers, Polynesians from the Marquesas. It is a plant that grows from sea level up to an elevation of fifteen hundred feet.

All varieties except for a few are vines with long runners and many roots, some of which enlarge to make what are, erroneously, called tubers.

Description

'Uala is a vigorously growing plant that spreads closely on the surface of the ground. Stem color differs with variety. Leaves are a dark green and vary in shape from heart shaped to five-lobed or angled with variety. The veins on the underside of the leaf may be green or colored. The pinkish lavender flowers are tubular below and spreading out above. The enlarged roots (so-called "tubers") grow primarily closely under the center of the plant. The colors of the skin, of the flesh just beneath the skin, and the flesh itself vary according to the variety, from white to cream to orange (flesh colors) and from cream to purple (skin colors).

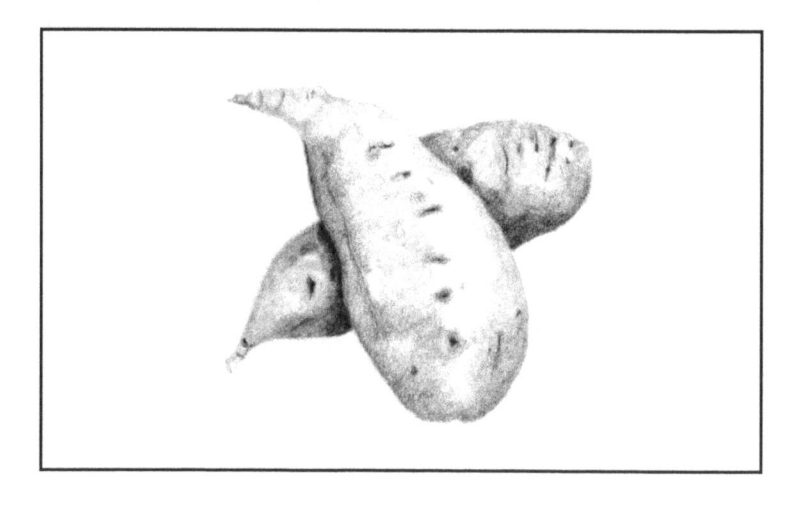

 General Uses

The main use of *'uala* was and still is for food. In old Hawai'i, the enlarged roots were baked in the *imu* (underground oven) for a staple food (important carbohydrate food), and the young leaves were steamed for a vegetable, much like our present-day "greens."

'*Uala* vines were also used to make an "undercushion" for *lau hala* mats in houses. And "cull" potatoes were fed to the pigs.

Medicinal Uses

 Ancient

Hawaiians had many varieties of *'uala*, and although most varieties could have been used for medicine, specific varieties were assigned to specific diseases.

To induce vomiting. For nausea "without a specific cause," i.e., to induce vomiting, perhaps after heavy eating, the variety *'uala huamoa* was used. This variety has a roundish leaf and swollen roots, with whitish skin and yellowish orange-red inner flesh like the yolk of an egg.

The flesh of the root was scraped, added to the tissue obtained by scraping the upper surfaces of *ki* leaves, and placed in sun-heated *niu* water. After thorough mixing of the above ingredients, the mixture was strained and drunk. The patient's throat was then tickled with a feather and vomiting thus induced.

Asthma. Several formulations for medicines to cure asthma are available. Following is one using the variety *'uala kihi*, which has a light-colored leaf with a red midrib on the underside, a whitish skin on the swollen root; a reddish purple outer flesh; and a yellow-orange inner flesh.

For asthma, the flesh of this sweet potato, plus *hinahina kū kahakai*; barks of *'ōhi'a 'ai* trunk and tap-root of *'uhaloa*; and juice from *kō honua'ula* were all mixed and pounded together to a mash. This concoction was strained and heated. While the patient lay down on his or her stomach, he or she drank the medicine twice a day, mornings and evenings, for five days. A great quantity of *ko'oko'olau* tea was also consumed during the five-day medication period.

Chest congestion. To free the chest (and stomach) from phlegm, the variety *'uala kiko nui* (characterized primarily by a large navel-like malformation on the swollen root, which gives this *'uala* its name) was used.

The flesh was grated and mixed with tissue scraped from the upper surface of ti leaves and fresh spring water. The whole was mixed, strained in the usual manner, and consumed as a drink. Along with this medication a lot of brackish water was also taken as a drink, and *mai'a lele* was eaten.

Insomnia. The inner flesh of the variety *'uala mōhihi* and of the *kalo* variety called *kalo pi'iali'i* were scraped and mixed with the slimy inner bark of *hau* and the fleshy stems of *kikawaiō*. Spring water was added and the mixture strained. The liquid was consumed in the evening. In the morning, an enema made from *noni* fruit that had been crushed, mashed, and cooked for one and a half hours, then strained and allowed to cool, was administered.

Increasing mother's milk supply. *'Uala* was also used to increase a nursing mother's milk supply. This was accomplished in the following manner and relates to the Hawaiians' belief that plant characteristics can be transferred to humans. An open *lei* made from *'uala* vines was hung around the mother's neck, or the breasts were beaten with a handful of vines, in the belief that the presence of the milky sap of *'uala* would induce the flow of the mother's milk.

'Uhaloa

Hawaiian name: *'Uhaloa*
Common name: Waltheria
Scientific name: *Waltheria indica* L.

 Description

'Uhaloa is a small, shrubby plant. Blunt-ovate (oblong) leaves are one to three-and-a-half inches long and velvety (due to a covering of short hairs) with toothed margins and conspicuous veins.

Flowers are small, with five yellow petals, and are densely clustered in the axils of the leaves. The fruits are tiny capsules that have two valves, each of which has one seed.

 Medicinal Uses

Ancient

Sore throat. The bark was removed from the taproot of *'uhaloa* and chewed to cure a sore throat. The fibrous residue left after chewing could be spat out. It was the sap that had the beneficial effect, an effect much like that of aspirin today. Bark was chewed three to four times a day, until the pain disappeared.

Asthma. Flowers, leaf buds and older leaves, and the bark from the taproot of *'uhaloa*, along with *'ala'ala wai nui pehu*; *kī* flowers; *pohepohe*, which grew in taro patches; tips of aerial roots of *hala*; dried *niu* flesh; mature *noni* fruit; and *kō kea* were mixed and pounded into a mash. The liquid in the mixture was squeezed into a gourd calabash and strained. The liquid was then heated and left to cool. When the liquid had cooled, the patient drank it while lying down. Enough of this medicine was made to allow for one dose a day for five days.

In postcontact days, after *he'i* (papaya, *Carica*

papaya) was introduced, juice squeezed from an "over-ripe" peeled papaya fruit was added to the above mixture before it was heated. *Ko'oko'olau* tea usually accompanied treatment with the *'uhaloa* medicine.

As a tonic. The bark of the taproot, flowers, and leaf buds and older leaves of *'uhaloa*; leaf buds and older leaves of *pōpolo*; meat from mature *niu*; mature *noni* fruit, and *kō kea* were mixed and pounded to a mash. The liquid was squeezed from the mash, strained, and heated. When the liquid had cooled, the patient drank it while lying on his or her abdomen. The water from a mature *niu* was taken as a drink and *mai'a iholena* was eaten.

The formulation was freshly made for each dosage. The medicine was taken morning and evening until five doses had been consumed.

ʻUlu

Hawaiian name: *ʻUlu*
Common name: Breadfruit
Scientific name: *Artocarpus altilis* S. Parkinson ex. Z

One variety of *'ulu* was brought from the Marquesas by the Polynesians who settled in Hawai'i. It is widespread throughout tropical Asia and the South Pacific islands. This is the only variety of breadfruit introduced by the Polynesians, and the fact that there is only one variety indicates that it was not an early introduction. The considerable number of other varieties of breadfruit found in Hawai'i today were introduced in postcontact times.

'Ulu is one of the most attractive tropical trees in the islands today, especially because of its beautiful foliage.

There are many legends involving this plant, in Hawai'i as well as throughout the rest of Polynesia.

 ## Description

The Hawaiian *'ulu* tree is tall, from thirty to sixty feet, with large, dark green leathery leaves, from one to three feet long, with the margins cut deeply into several blunt lobes; such leaves add to the attractiveness of the tree as a whole.

Female and male inflorescences grow separately on the same tree. The female inflorescence consists of many small flowers, pressed together and attached to a central "stem" to form a compact round "head." The male inflorescence is made up of many small male flowers closely appressed (lying close to or pressed against something) in a stiff, club-shaped spike, chartreuse when immature, turning to a brownish tan when it is mature and falls. Both the male and female inflorescences are enclosed in sheaths, which are shed as the inflorescences develop.

The fruit, which develops from the female inflorescence, is round in the Hawaiian variety, about six to

eight inches in diameter. Its "skin" is a bright pea-green when immature, changing to a dull or tannish green when mature. The "skin" is tough and somewhat warty, patterned with the angled outlines of the bases of the female flowers. The flesh consists of a sweetish pulp that is somewhat mealy.

The Hawaiian variety has no seeds.

  General Uses

'Ulu had many uses in old Hawai'i. The trunk was used for small, coastal-plying canoes and *poi*-pounding boards; the inner fibrous bark was used to make *kapa* of a quality preferred by Tahitians but considered too coarse and inferior to *wauke* (paper mulberry, *Broussonetia papyrifera*) by the Hawaiians; the milky sap was used in caulking seams in canoes, and for

chewing gum; the bracts enclosing young leaves and the inflorescence made a very fine sandpaper; and the fruit, baked in an *imu,* was eaten as a starchy food or was pounded into a *poi* (not very popular because of its rapid fermentation), or mixed with *niu* cream to make a kind of pudding.

Medicinal Uses

Ancient

Infected sore. An *'opihi* shell full of the milky sap of *'ulu* and one *'opihi* shell full of very finely powdered *'ahu'awa* were mixed together and added to the kernels ("meat") of eight unripe *kukui* nuts that had been wrapped in *kī* leaves, broiled over charcoal embers, and when cool, pounded to a very fine mash. A large amount of powder made from *lama* was then added, and all ingredients mixed well, until smooth. This concoction was applied to the sore twice a day, in the morning and in the evening, until the sore healed.

Before each new application, the sore was washed with the following liquid: four pieces of bark from *'ahakea* were pounded to a mash, a small, long-necked water gourd full of fresh spring water was added, and this mixture was cooked by adding four red-hot stones. The strained liquid is dark.

No specific formulations for medicine containing *'ulu* plant material exist, but mention has been made that the sap was also used for medication for rashes and wounds as well.

 ## Contemporary

The sap from *'ulu* is still used to some extent for healing cuts, cracked or chapped skin, scratches, and sores around the mouth.

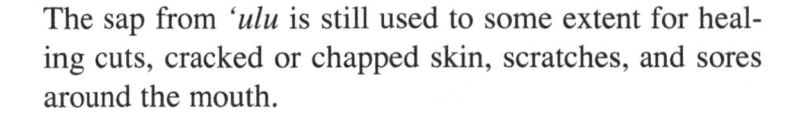

Wauke

Hawaiian name: *Wauke*
Common name: Paper mulberry
Scientific name: *Broussonetia papyrifera* (L.) Venten.

Wauke is a Polynesian-introduced plant; i.e., it was brought by the first settlers, who came from the Marquesas. Its common name, paper mulberry, comes from the paperlike texture of beaten fibers and is reflected in its species name, *papyrifera,* referring to the first "paper" made from papyrus.

Description

Belonging to the mulberry family, *wauke* is a small, fast-growing, shrubby tree, up to fifteen feet tall.

The leaves, slightly heart shaped, are up to eight inches long and up to five inches wide. The margins are either entire or two- or three-lobed, all three forms sometimes occurring on the same plant. The upper surface is rough and the lower surface "woolly." The petiole is up to four inches long, with large stipules.

Male and female inflorescences occur on different (separate) plants. The female flowers form a head about an inch in diameter with long stigmas (female parts) and hairy bracts. Mature fruit is scarce.

General Uses

Wauke was cultivated by the ancient Hawaiians, its principal use being to make *kapa*, the fabric beaten from its inner stem bark.

Medicinal Uses

Ancient

Thrush. Young shoots or suckers of *wauke* were used, the formulation depending upon the age of the child: four shoots from ages ten days to two months; eight shoots until four months; twelve shoots until eight months; sixteen shoots until one year, after which no more were given. No instructions were given as to preparation or dosages.

Contemporary

The leaves of *wauke*, both fresh and dry, are used today primarily in a tea as a tonic.

Glossary of Botanical Terms

achene a small, hard, dry fruit having one seed with a thin outer covering that does not burst when mature

annual a plant that grows for only a year

anther the pollen-bearing part of the stamen

appressed lying close to or pressed against something

awn a bristly hair

axil the angle between a leaf and the stem

blunt-ovate oblong

bract a leaflike flower part

calyx the outer row of flower parts, usually green, made up of the sepals

compound (leaf) made up of smaller units called "leaflets"

corm a food-storing underground stem

corolla the petals cup

cultivar a cultivated, as opposed to wild, variety

drupe a fleshy fruit or fruitlet usually containing a single hard stone enclosing a seed

endemic native to one place only

entire (leaf margins) without teeth or notches

globose rounded

haustoria rootlike outgrowths that obtain food from a host plant

indigenous native to more than one place, with a character unique to each area

inflorescence a flower cluster or head

internode a part of a stem between two nodes

introduced not native

meristematic growing

native originating in its place of growth. See **endemic** and **indigenous**.

node the point on a stem where a leaf is, or has been, attached

ovate-lanceolate egg-shaped, longer than wide, with a tapering tip

ovoid somewhat elongated

panicle a loose cluster of flowers

pedicel a stalk

perennial a plant that lives for a few years

perfect having both female and male parts

petiole the leaf stem

phyllode a flattened leaf stem

pinna a branchlet of a leaf composed of branchlets arranged on either side of a common axis, like a feather

pistil the female organ of a flower, including the stigma, style, and ovary

rhizome an underground stem

sepal one of the separate parts forming the calyx

serrated (leaf margins) toothed or notched

sessile (leaf) without a stalk; attached directly at its base to a branch

simple (leaf) occuring singly

stamen the pollen-producing male organ of a flower

stigma the part of the pistil on which the pollen is deposited

stipule a leaflike structure at the base of the leaf stem

syncarp a fleshy compound fruit composed of the fruits of several flowers

tepals sepals and petals that are similar in appearance

woolly covered with hairs

xerophytic adapted to grow in hot, dry areas

Bibliography

Information on present-day use of medicinal herbs has come from many sources, both printed and oral. Having been born and lived in Hawai'i, I have acquired this information from many people as well as from my reading. Martha Noyes has added information as well.

The following two books are my primary sources for information about early use of Hawaiian medicinal herbs.

Chun, Malcolm Naea, trans. and ed. *Native Hawaiian Medicines.* Honolulu: First People's Productions, 1994.

Handy, E.S. Craighill, Mary Kawena Pukui, and Katherine Livermore. *Outline of Hawaiian Physical Therapeutics.* Honolulu: Bernice P. Bishop Museum, 1934.

Index

Printed in the USA
CPSIA information can be obtained
at www.ICGtesting.com
CBHW031731160524
8583CB00001B/62